Daily Word Ladders
and Vocabulary Builder
for Grades K-1

ISBN: 978-1-953149-59-6
Copyright © 2024 by Polymath Panda

This Book Belongs To:

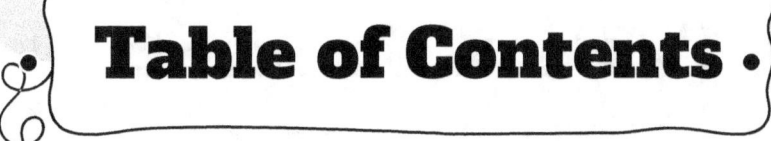

Table of Contents

Table of Contents

We're So Glad You're Here!

Dear Parents and Teachers,

Are you ready to embark on a word-filled adventure with your young learners? This book is packed with over 100 engaging activities designed to turn reading, spelling, and phonics into a fun and exciting game. With each Word Ladder, your child or student will discover new words, boost their literacy skills, and have a blast along the way!

What are Word Ladders?

Word Ladders are like magical word puzzles. Starting with a simple word like cat, children change one letter at a time to create new words, such as bat, hat, and mat. Each step up the ladder is a new challenge that helps them climb higher in their word skills.

Why You and Your Child/Student Will Love This Book:

- **Quick and Fun:** Each Word Ladder takes just a few minutes to complete, perfect for short, focused learning sessions.
- **Learn While You Play:** These activities enhance reading, spelling, and phonics skills in an interactive way.
- **Puzzles and Games:** Kids will love the game-like feel, making learning enjoyable and effective.

How to Use This Book:

- **Top of the Page:** Each page starts with a Word Ladder activity where children read clues and change letters to form new words.
- **Bottom of the Page:** The second half includes additional fun activities like alphabetical order games and high-frequency word practice to reinforce learning.
- **100 Pages of Fun:** Provides a wide variety of ladders and exercises to keep learning fresh and exciting.

With each new word, your child is not just learning—they're becoming a word wizard. Let's see how high they can go on the Word Ladder!

BONUS COLORING BOOK!

QR Code in the Back of the Book

Building with Mat

Activity 1 — Word Ladder

1. Read the clues and write each word on the ladder.
2. Start at the bottom and climb to the top of the ladder.

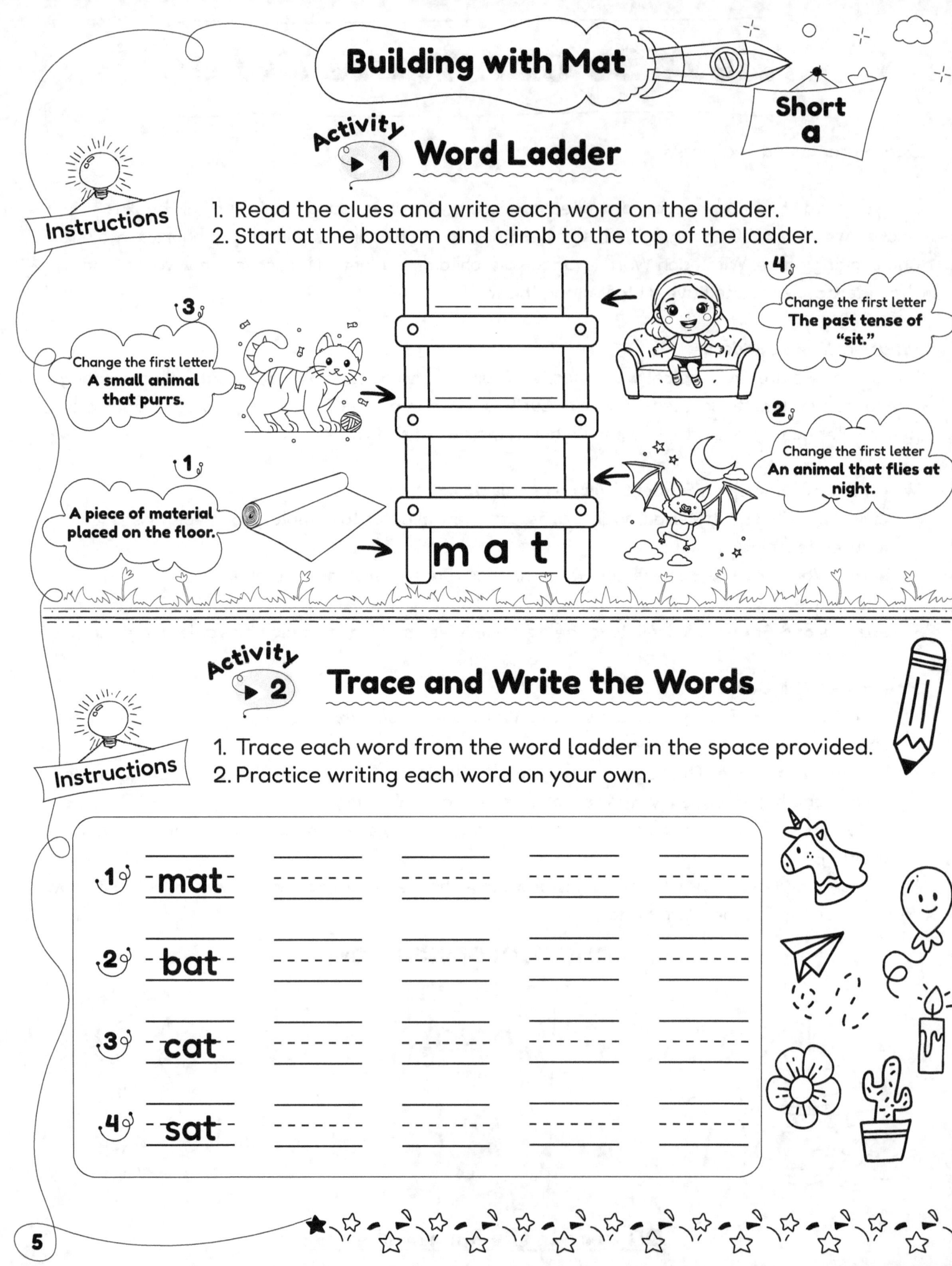

3 Change the first letter
A small animal that purrs.

1 A piece of material placed on the floor.

4 Change the first letter
The past tense of "sit."

2 Change the first letter
An animal that flies at night.

m a t

Activity 2 — Trace and Write the Words

1. Trace each word from the word ladder in the space provided.
2. Practice writing each word on your own.

1 mat ------ ------ ------ ------
2 bat ------ ------ ------ ------
3 cat ------ ------ ------ ------
4 sat ------ ------ ------ ------

Best Lad

Activity 1 — Word Ladder

1. Read the clues and write each word on the ladder.
2. Start at the bottom and climb to the top of the ladder.

4 Change the first letter
Feeling very angry

3 Change the first letter
Feeling unhappy

2 Change the first letter
Another word for father

1 A young boy

l a d

Activity 2 — Sort Words into Categories

Write each word in the correct category.

Word Bank

lad
mad
sad
dad

Feelings	Person

6

Rat-tastic Rhymes

Activity 1 — Word Ladder

1. Read the clues and write each word on the ladder.
2. Start at the bottom and climb to the top of the ladder.

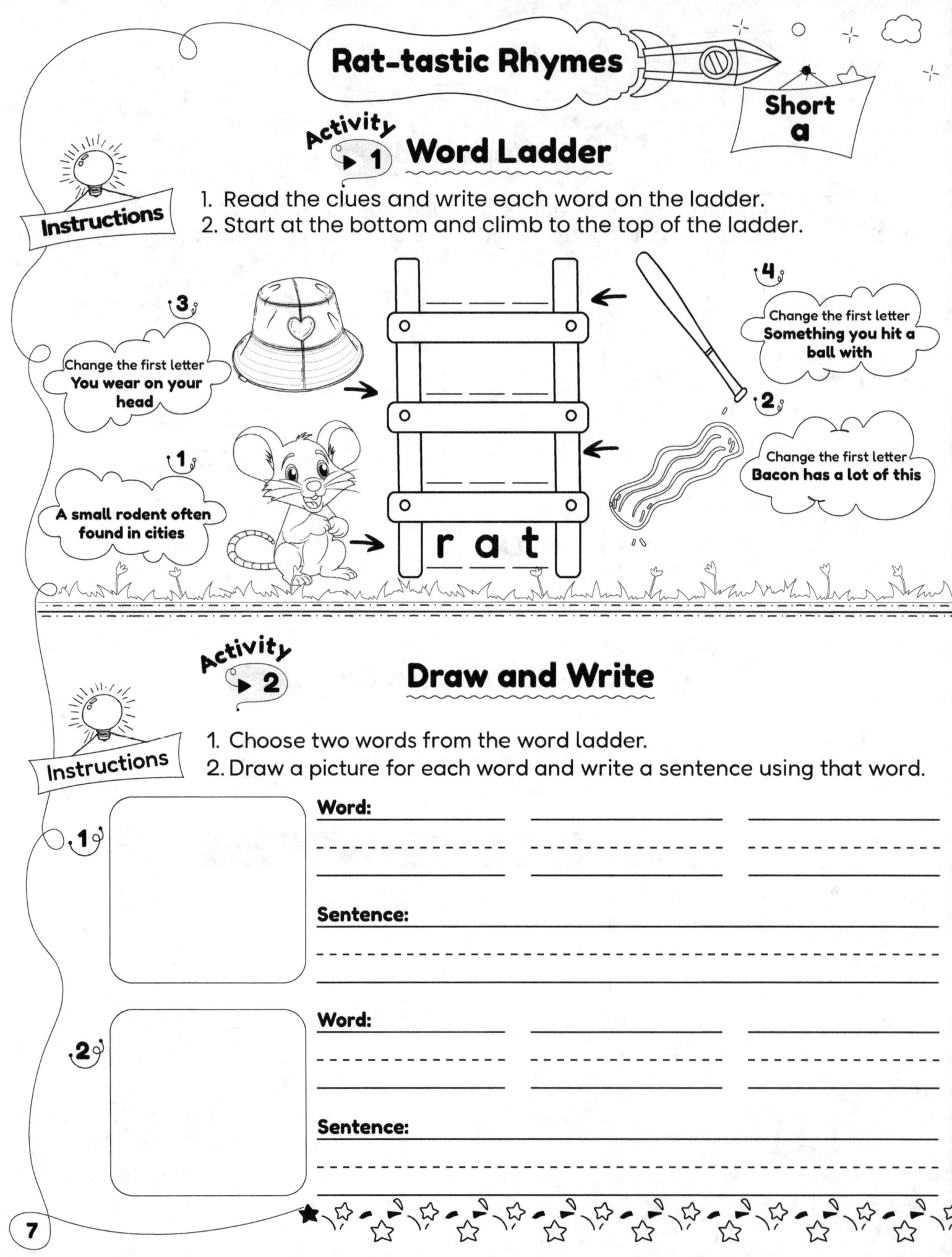

3 Change the first letter
You wear on your head

1 A small rodent often found in cities

4 Change the first letter
Something you hit a ball with

2 Change the first letter
Bacon has a lot of this

r a t

Activity 2 — Draw and Write

1. Choose two words from the word ladder.
2. Draw a picture for each word and write a sentence using that word.

1

Word: _____ _____ _____

Sentence: _____

2

Word: _____ _____ _____

Sentence: _____

Go with Zap

Activity 1 — Word Ladder

Instructions
1. Read the clues and write each word on the ladder.
2. Start at the bottom and climb to the top of the ladder.

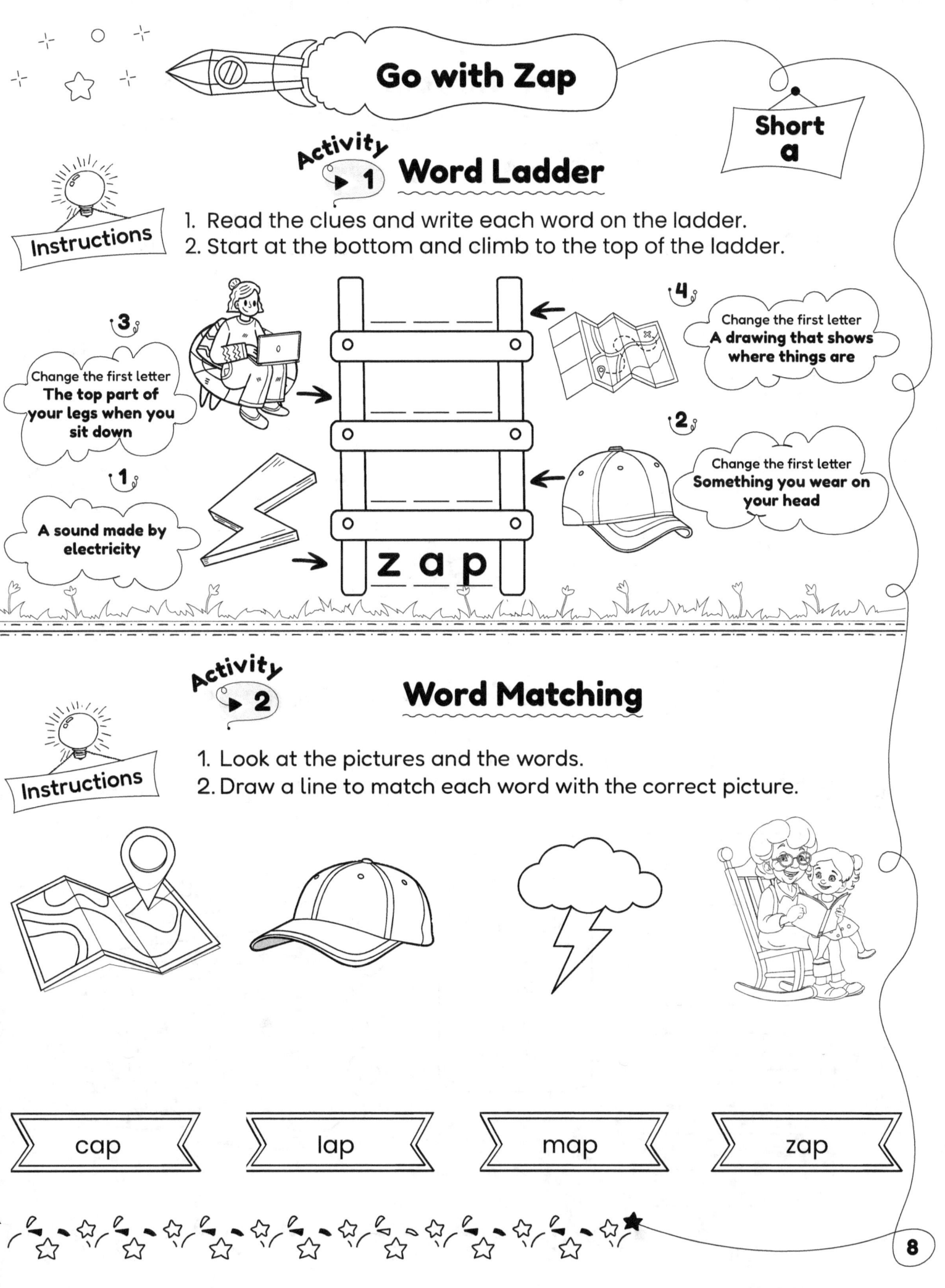

3 Change the first letter
The top part of your legs when you sit down

1 A sound made by electricity

4 Change the first letter
A drawing that shows where things are

2 Change the first letter
Something you wear on your head

z a p

Activity 2 — Word Matching

Instructions
1. Look at the pictures and the words.
2. Draw a line to match each word with the correct picture.

cap   lap   map   zap

8

In the Jam

Short a

Activity 1 — Word Ladder

Instructions

1. Read the clues and write each word on the ladder.
2. Start at the bottom and climb to the top of the ladder.

3. Change the first letter
Meat from the upper part of a pig's leg.

4. Change the first letter
A male sheep.

1. A sweet spread made from fruit.

2. Change the first letter
A barrier that stops the flow of water.

j a m

Activity 2 — Alphabetical Order Exercises

Instructions

1. Look at the list of words from the word ladder.
2. Write the words in alphabetical order in the spaces provided.

1. _____
2. _____
3. _____
4. _____

Word Bank
ram
jam
ham
dam

Keep It in a Bag

Activity 1 Word Ladder

Instructions

1. Read the clues and write each word on the ladder.
2. Start at the bottom and climb to the top of the ladder.

3 Change the first letter **A label attached to something.**

4 Change the first letter **To move back and forth, like a dog's tail.**

1 **Used to carry things.**

2 Change the first letter **A piece of old cloth.**

b a g

Activity 2 Practice High-Frequency Words

Instructions

1. Look at each flashcard with a sight word.
2. Read the word aloud.
3. Practice writing the word in the space provided.

tag

bag

wag

rag

Jar for Fun

Activity 1 — Word Ladder

1. Read the clues and write each word on the ladder.
2. Start at the bottom and climb to the top of the ladder.

3. Change the first letter
A long, rigid piece of wood or metal

1. **A container made of glass or plastic**

4. Change the first letter
A long distance away

2. Change the first letter
A vehicle that moves on wheels

j a r

Activity 2 — Simple Word Search

1. Find words from the word ladder within the grid.
2. Circle the words when you find them

R	G	R	X	B
E	A	C	A	R
B	H	J	R	N
U	Z	J	A	V
P	A	A	F	T

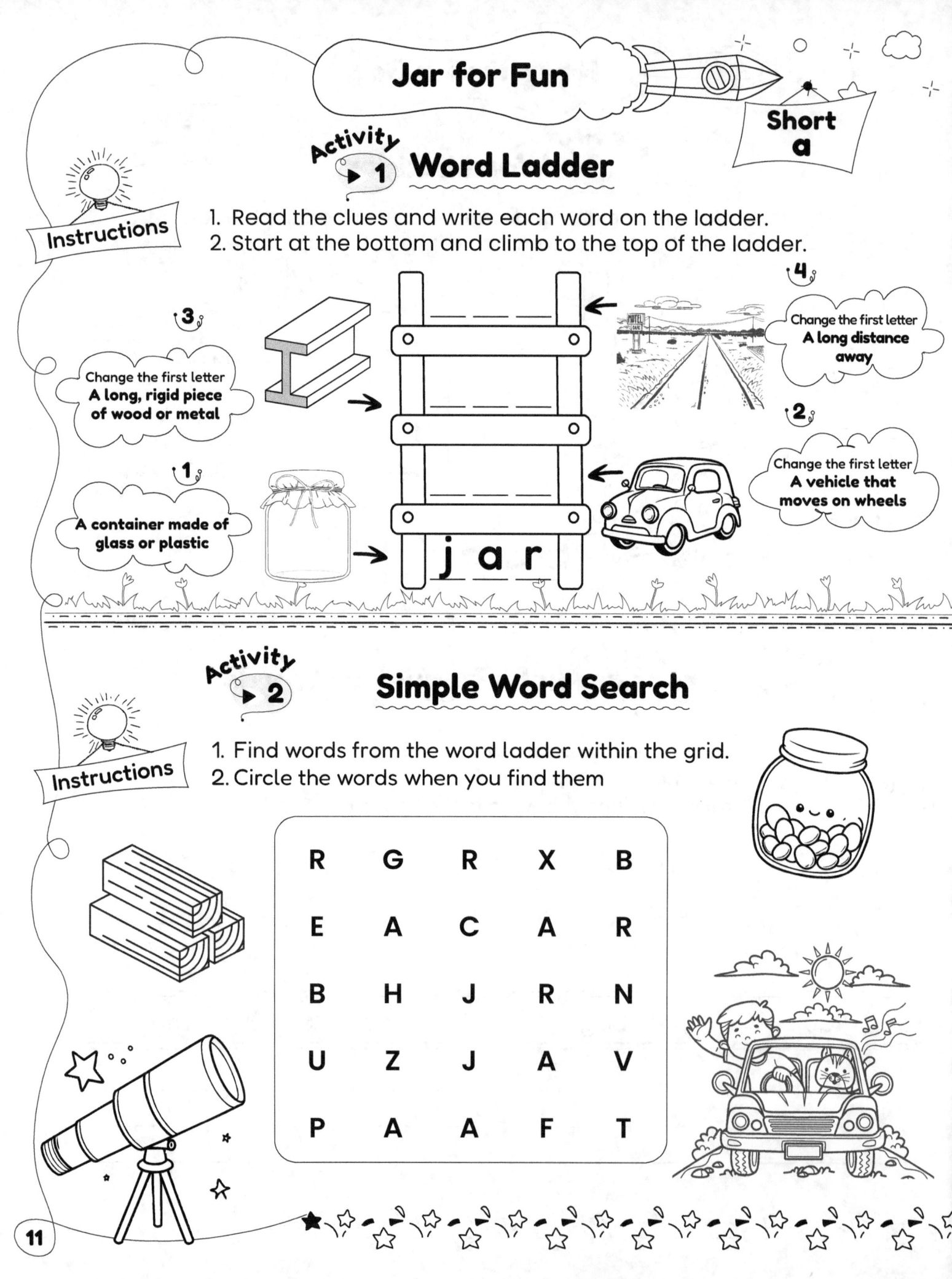

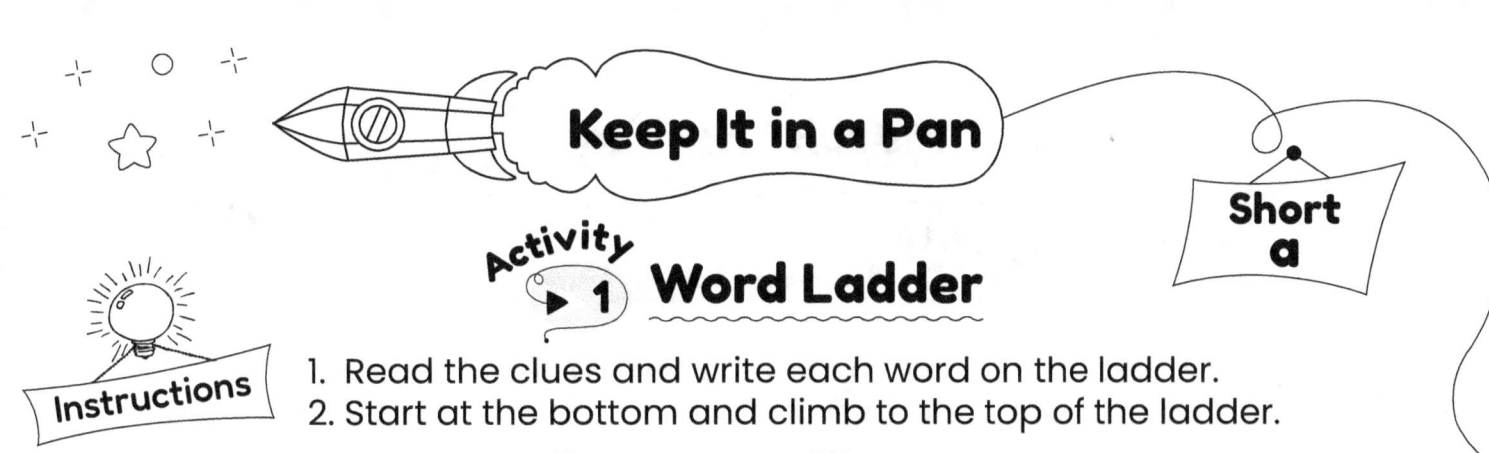

Keep It in a Pan

Activity ▶ 1 Word Ladder

Instructions
1. Read the clues and write each word on the ladder.
2. Start at the bottom and climb to the top of the ladder.

3. Change the first letter — A container for liquids or food

4. Change the first letter — An adult male human

2. Change the first letter — A device that moves air

1. A container used for cooking

p a n

Activity ▶ 2 Decode the Secret Words

Instructions
1. Use the key (a=1, b=2, etc.) to decode each number into a letter.
2. Write the decoded word in the space provided.

v	b	c	d	e	f	g	h	i	j	k	l	m	n	o	p	q	r	s	t	u	v	w	x	y	z
1	2	3	4	5	6	7	8	9	10	11	12	13	14	15	16	17	18	19	20	21	22	23	24	25	26

1. 13-1-14: A grown-up boy

_____

2. 16-1-14: You cook food in this on the stove.

_____

3. 6-1-14: This keeps you cool on a hot day

_____

4. 3-1-14: You might find soup or soda in this

_____

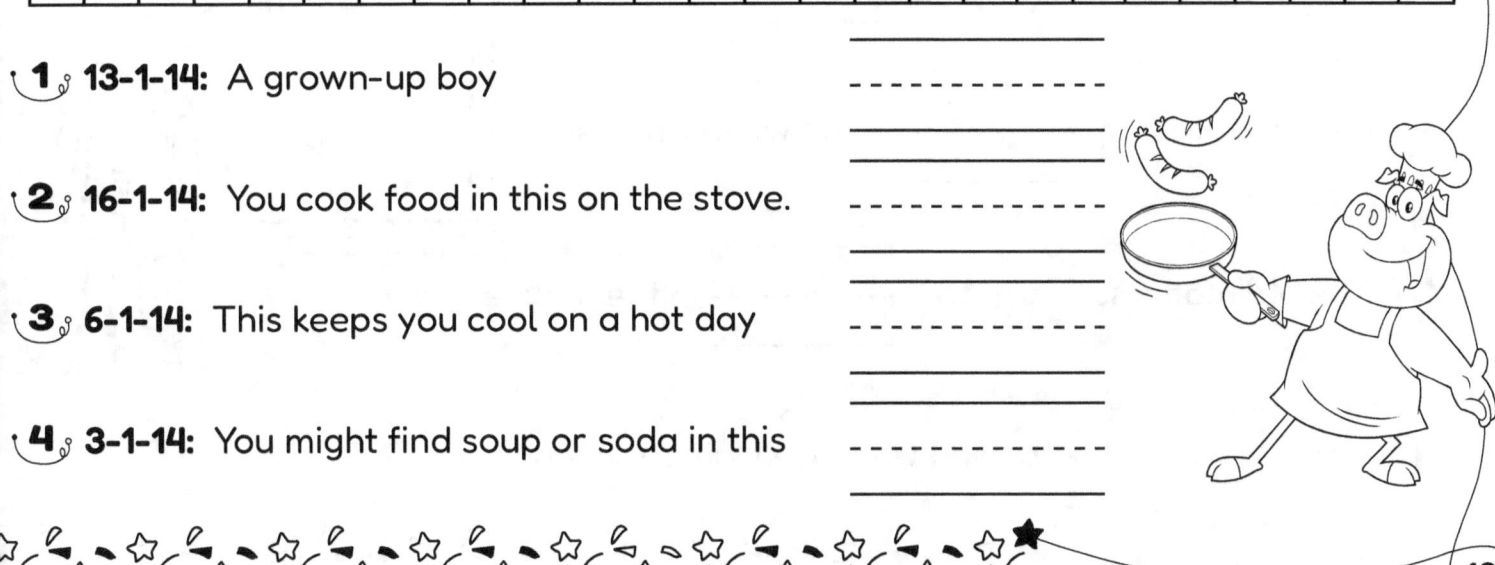

12

Match the Tag

Activity 1 — Word Ladder

Instructions

1. Read the clues and write each word on the ladder.
2. Start at the bottom and climb to the top of the ladder.

3 Replace 'n' with 's'
To sink or droop down

1 **A label attached to something**

4 Replace 's' with 'l'
To fall behind

2 Replace 't' with 'n'
To bother someone repeatedly

t a g

Activity 2 — Fill in the Blanks

Instructions

1. Complete each sentence with a word from the word bank.
2. Write the word in the blank space.

1. The present had a nice ----------- on it.

2. My sister likes to ----------- me when I'm busy.

3. The old mattress began to ----------- in the middle.

4. Don't ----------- behind when we walk to school.

Word Bank
lag
tag
nag
sag

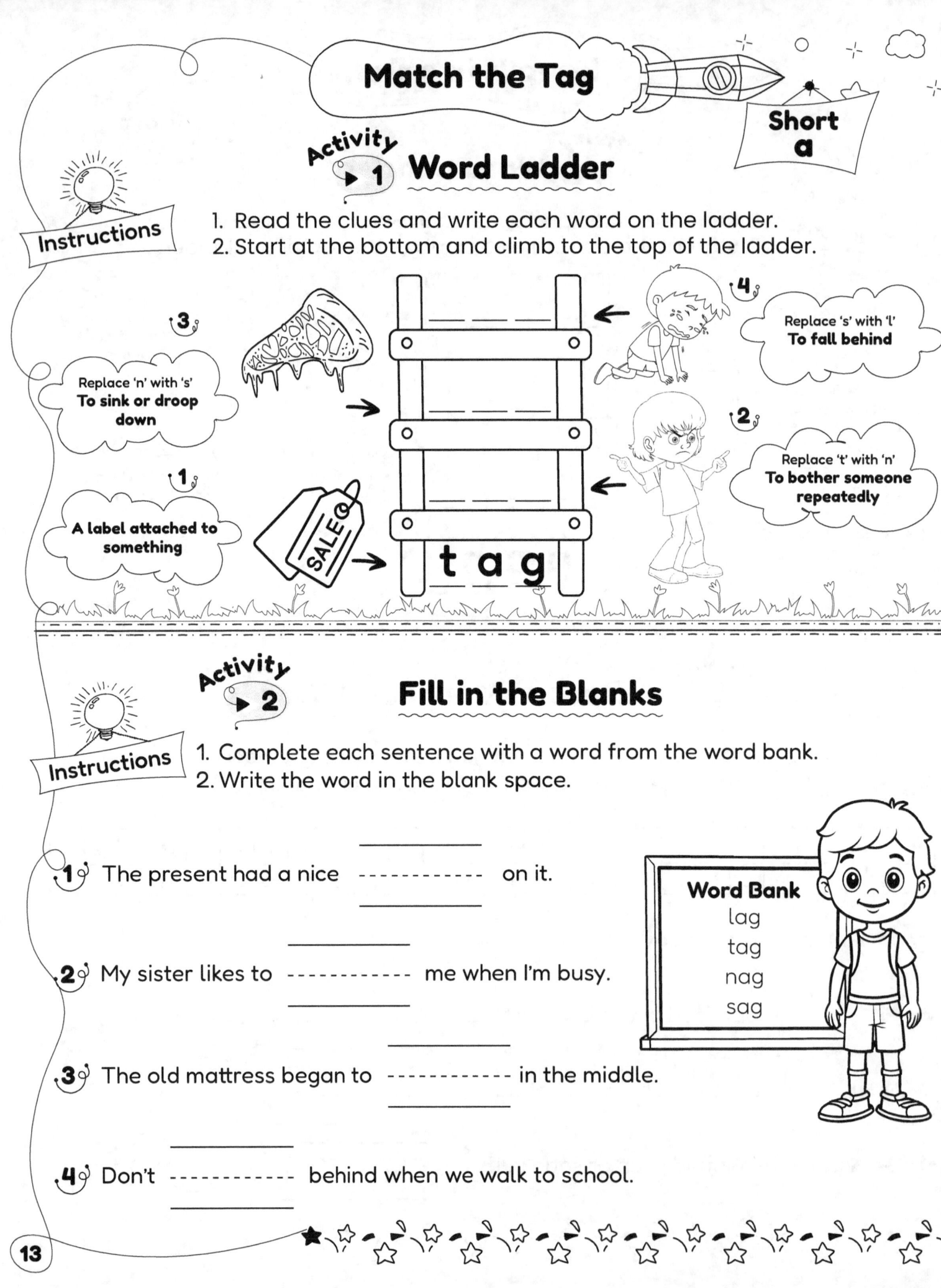

13

Pan Fun

Activity 1 — Word Ladder

Instructions

1. Read the clues and write each word on the ladder.
2. Start at the bottom and climb to the top of the ladder.

3. Change the first letter
A type of vehicle

4. Change the first letter
A light brown skin color

1. Something you cook in.

2. Change the first letter
A container for holding liquids or food.

p a n

Activity 2 — Rhyming Words Activity

Instructions

Draw a picture of your favorite word that rhymes with 'pan'.

pan

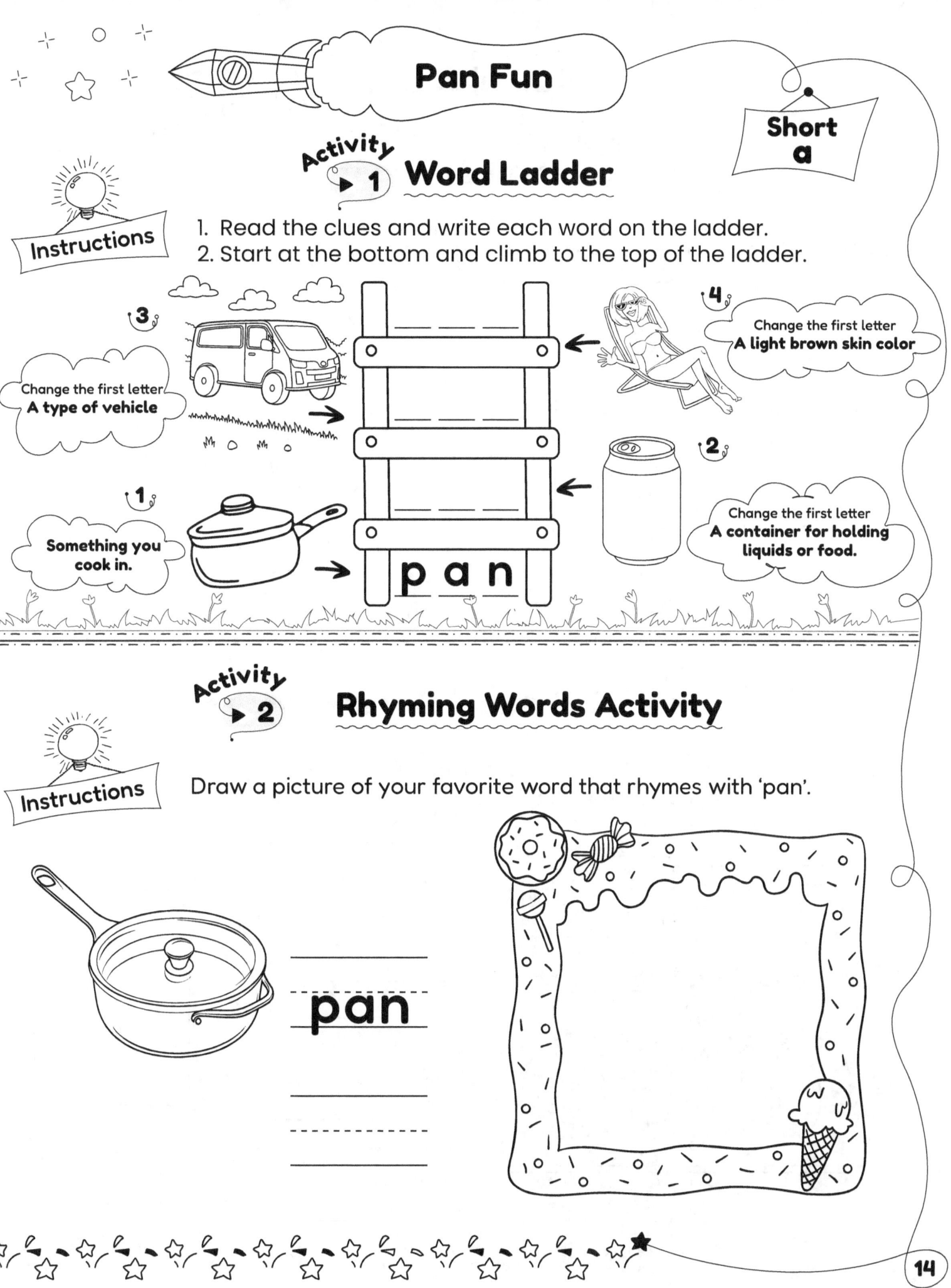

14

Play with Cab

Activity 1 Word Ladder

Instructions

1. Read the clues and write each word on the ladder.
2. Start at the bottom and climb to the top of the ladder.

3 Change the first letter
A place where scientists work

4 Change the first letter
A small amount of something

1 **A car you pay to ride in.**

2 Change the first letter
A small flap or piece that sticks out

c a b

Activity 2 Alphabetical Order Exercises

Instructions

1. Look at the list of words from the word ladder.
2. Write the words in alphabetical order in the spaces provided.

1 - - - - - - - - - -

2 - - - - - - - - - -

3 - - - - - - - - - -

4 - - - - - - - - - -

Word Bank
tab
cab
dab
lab

15

Wax On, Wax Off!

Activity 1 Word Ladder

Instructions
1. Read the clues and write each word on the ladder.
2. Start at the bottom and climb to the top of the ladder.

4 Replace 'w' with 'f'
A machine that sends documents over the phone line

3 Replace 't' with 'w'
A substance used for candles

2 Replace 'v' with 't'
Money you pay to the government

1 **A shortened word for vaccine**

v a x

Activity 2 Identify Consonants and Vowels

Instructions
1. Look at the words from the word ladder.
2. Circle the consonants in each word.
3. Underline the vowel in each word.

1 t a x   **2** v a x   **3** f a x   **4** w a x

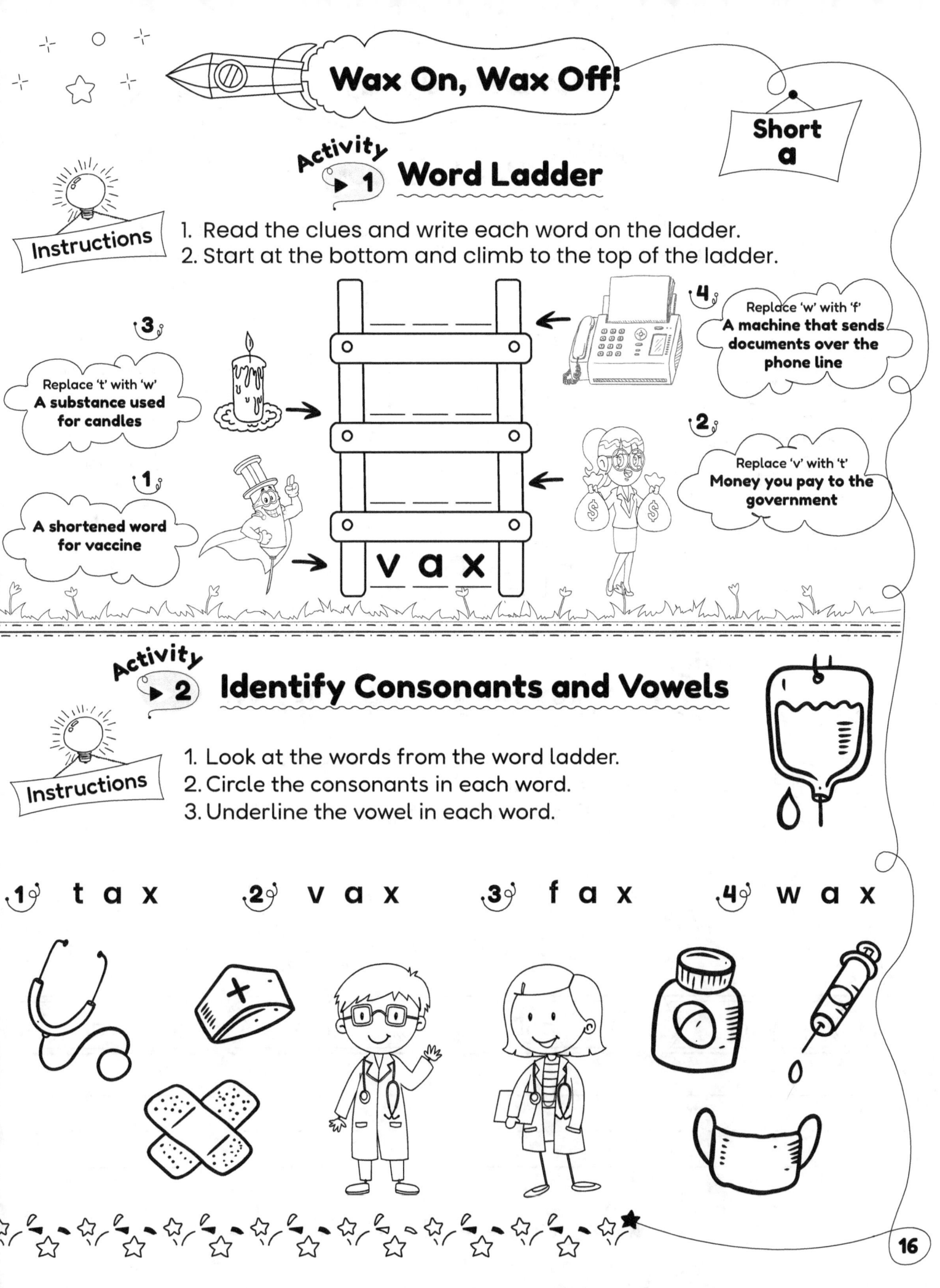

16

Pat's Word Play

Activity 1 — Word Ladder

1. Read the clues and write each word on the ladder.
2. Start at the bottom and climb to the top of the ladder.

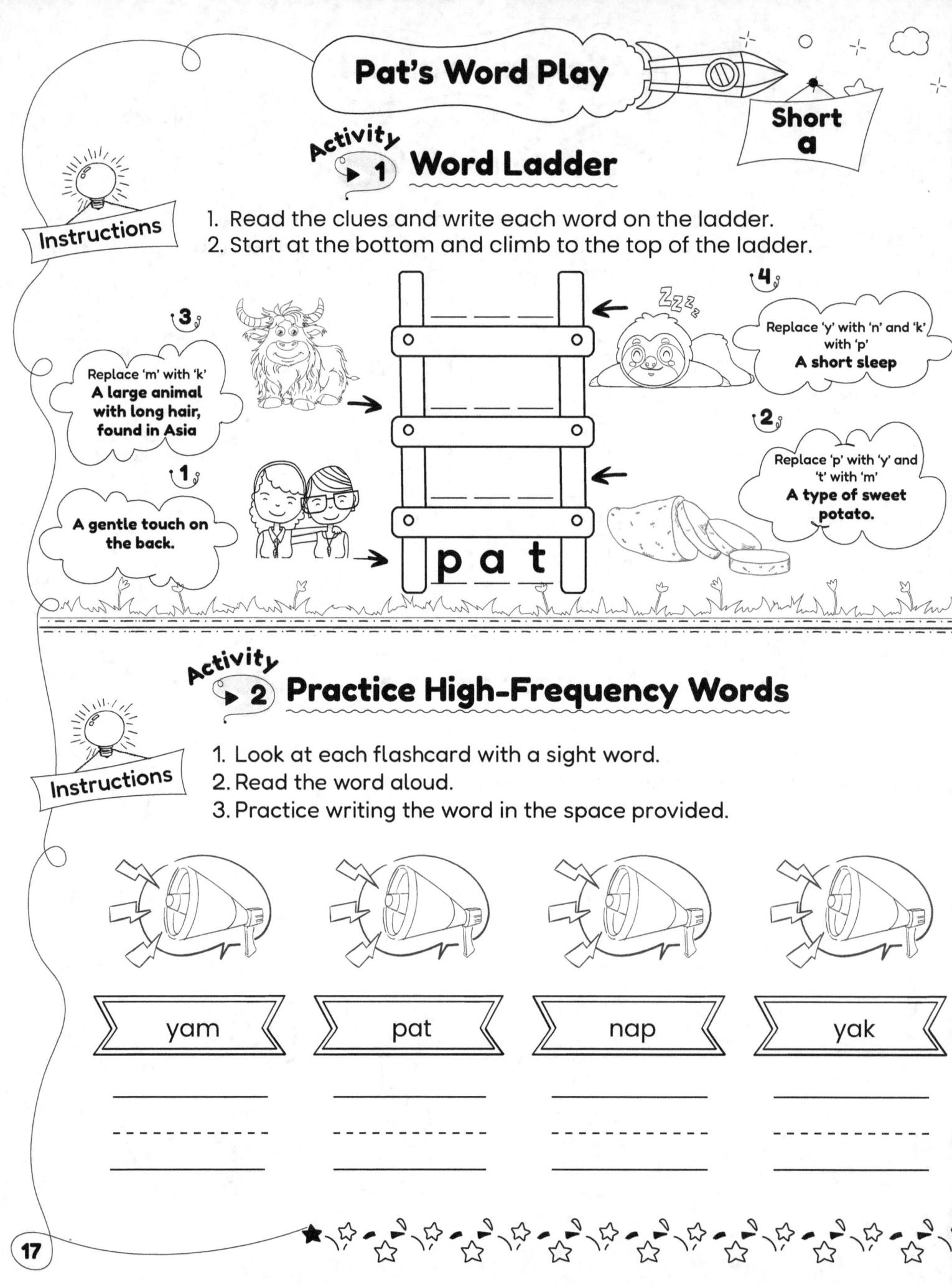

4 Replace 'y' with 'n' and 'k' with 'p'
A short sleep

3 Replace 'm' with 'k'
A large animal with long hair, found in Asia

2 Replace 'p' with 'y' and 't' with 'm'
A type of sweet potato.

1 **A gentle touch on the back.**

p a t

Activity 2 — Practice High-Frequency Words

1. Look at each flashcard with a sight word.
2. Read the word aloud.
3. Practice writing the word in the space provided.

| yam | pat | nap | yak |

Close the Gap

Activity ▶ 1 Word Ladder

1. Read the clues and write each word on the ladder.
2. Start at the bottom and climb to the top of the ladder.

3 Replace 'n' with 'r'
A type of music with rhyming lyrics

1 Something you turn to get water.

4 Replace 'r' with 'g'
Be careful not to fall into this.

2 Replace 't' with 'n'
A short sleep

t a p

Activity ▶ 2 Alphabetical Order Exercises

1. Look at the list of words from the word ladder.
2. Write the words in alphabetical order in the spaces provided.

1 - - - - - - - - -

2 - - - - - - - - -

3 - - - - - - - - -

4 - - - - - - - - -

Word Bank
nap
gap
rap
tap

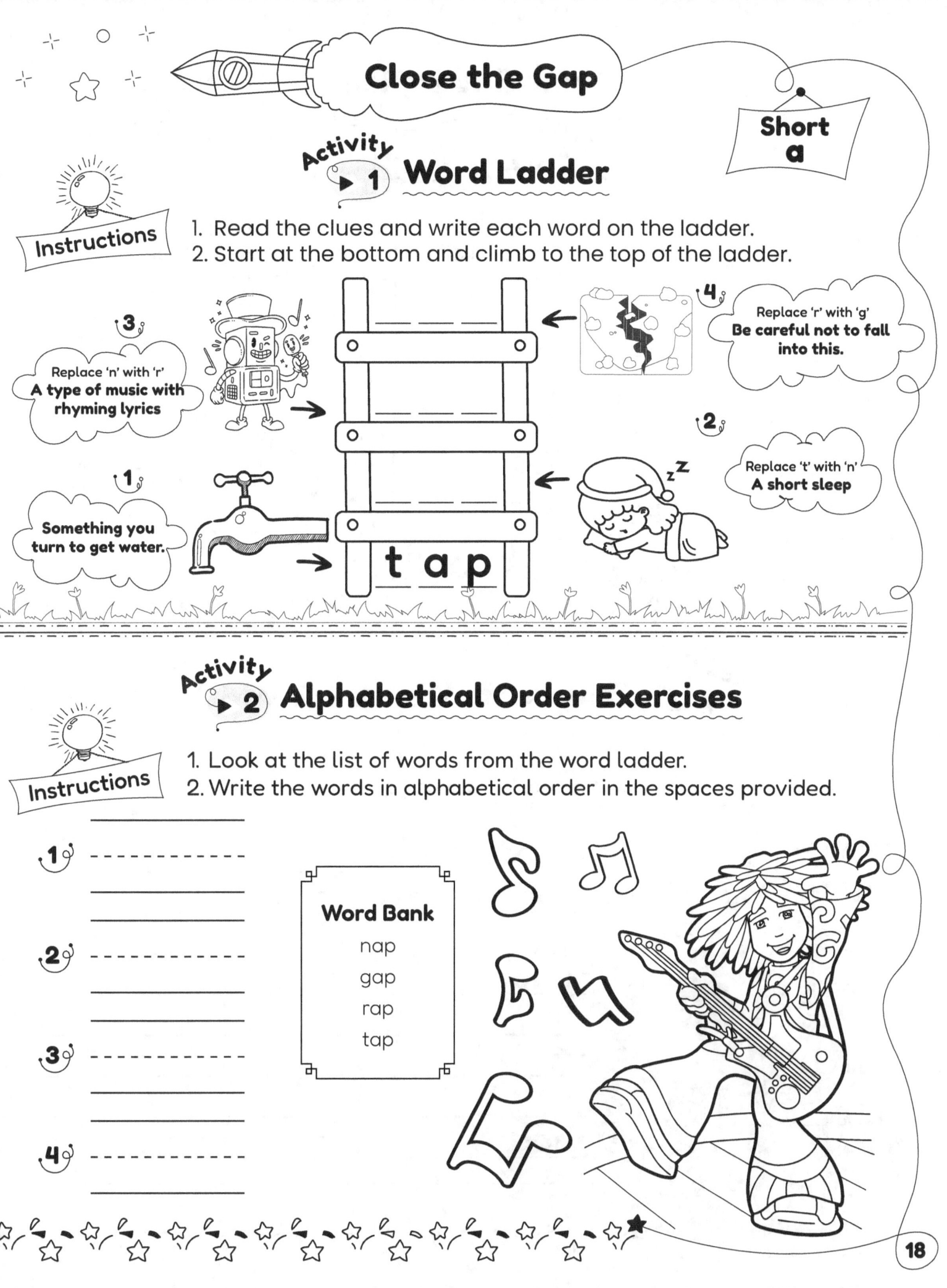

From Bad to Rad

Activity 1 — Word Ladder

1. Read the clues and write each word on the ladder.
2. Start at the bottom and climb to the top of the ladder.

4 Change 'f' to 'r'
Meaning awesome or cool.

3 Change 'p' to 'f'
Something that is very popular for a short time

2 Change 'b' to 'p'
A cushion or a small notebook

1 Not good

b a d

Activity 2 — Trace and Write the Words

1. Trace each word from the word ladder in the space provided.
2. Practice writing each word on your own.

1. rad
2. pad
3. fad
4. bad

Building with Leg

Activity 1 Word Ladder

Instructions

1. Read the clues and write each word on the ladder.
2. Start at the bottom and climb to the top of the ladder.

4 Change 'b' to 'm'
A name (short for Megan)

3 Change 'p' to 'b'
To ask for something desperately

2 Change 'l' to 'p'
A small hook or pin.

1 **A part of the body used for walking.**

l e g

Activity 2 Alphabetical Order Exercises

Instructions

1. Look at the list of words from the word ladder.
2. Write the words in alphabetical order in the spaces provided.

1 _ _ _ _ _ _ _ _ _ _

2 _ _ _ _ _ _ _ _ _ _

3 _ _ _ _ _ _ _ _ _ _

4 _ _ _ _ _ _ _ _ _ _

Word Bank
leg
peg
beg
meg

Ten-der Word

Activity 1 — Word Ladder

Instructions

1. Read the clues and write each word on the ladder.
2. Start at the bottom and climb to the top of the ladder.

3 Change the first letter
The number after nine

1 A tool for writing.

4 Change the first letter
A female chicken

2 Change the first letter
Plural of man

p e n

Activity 2 — Match Words to Pictures

Instructions

1. Match each picture with the correct word from the word ladder.
2. Write the correct word below each picture.

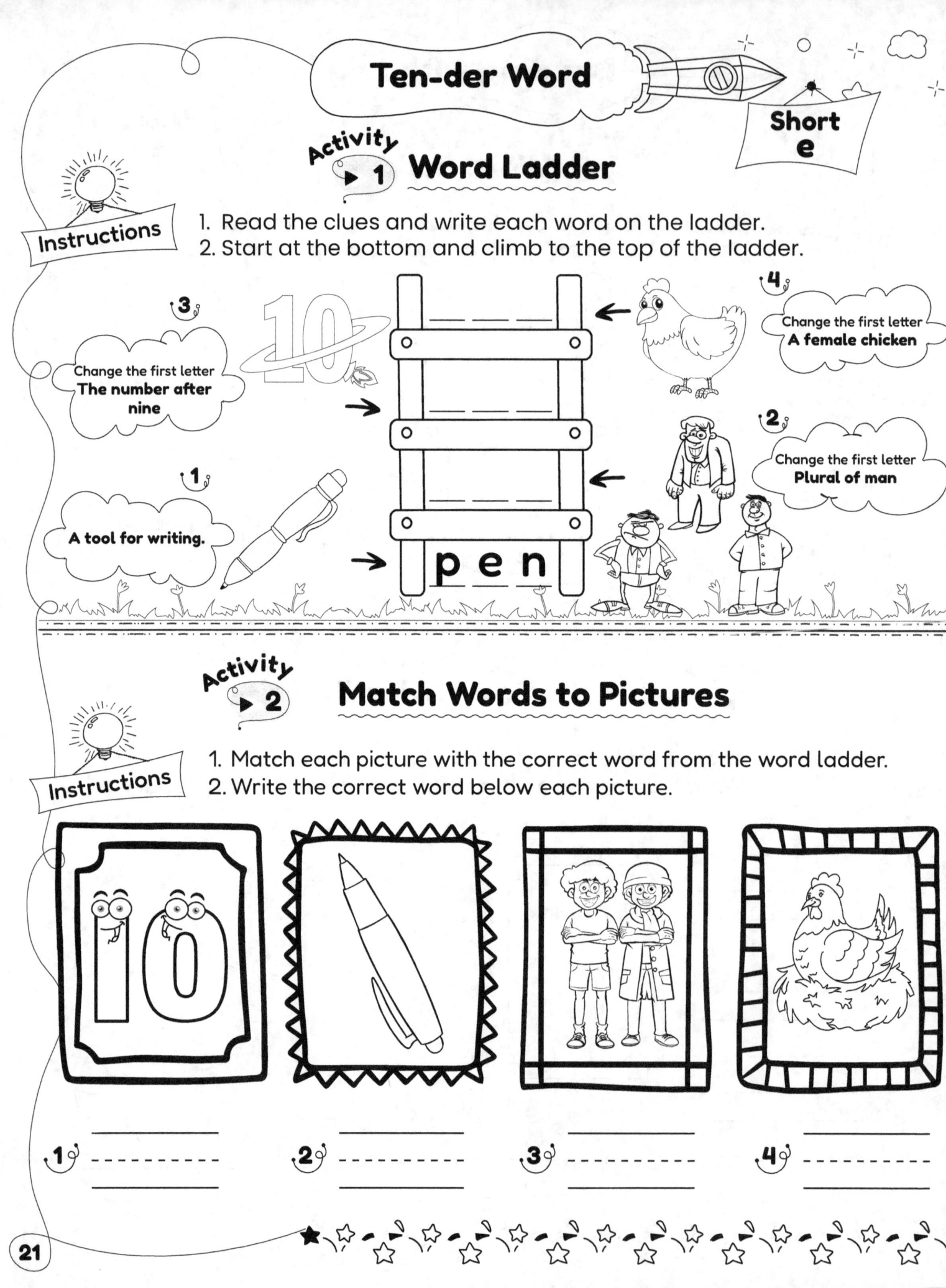

1) _ _ _ _ _ _ _ _ _

2) _ _ _ _ _ _ _ _ _

3) _ _ _ _ _ _ _ _ _

4) _ _ _ _ _ _ _ _ _

Bed of Words

Activity ▶ 1 Word Ladder

Instructions
1. Read the clues and write each word on the ladder.
2. Start at the bottom and climb to the top of the ladder.

3 Change the first letter
A color

4 Change the first letter
To get married

1 A piece of furniture
for sleeping

2 Change the first letter
Past tense of lead

l a d

Activity ▶ 2 Sort Words into Categories

Instructions Write each word in the correct category

Word Bank

| led | red | wed | bed |

Furniture	Actions	Color

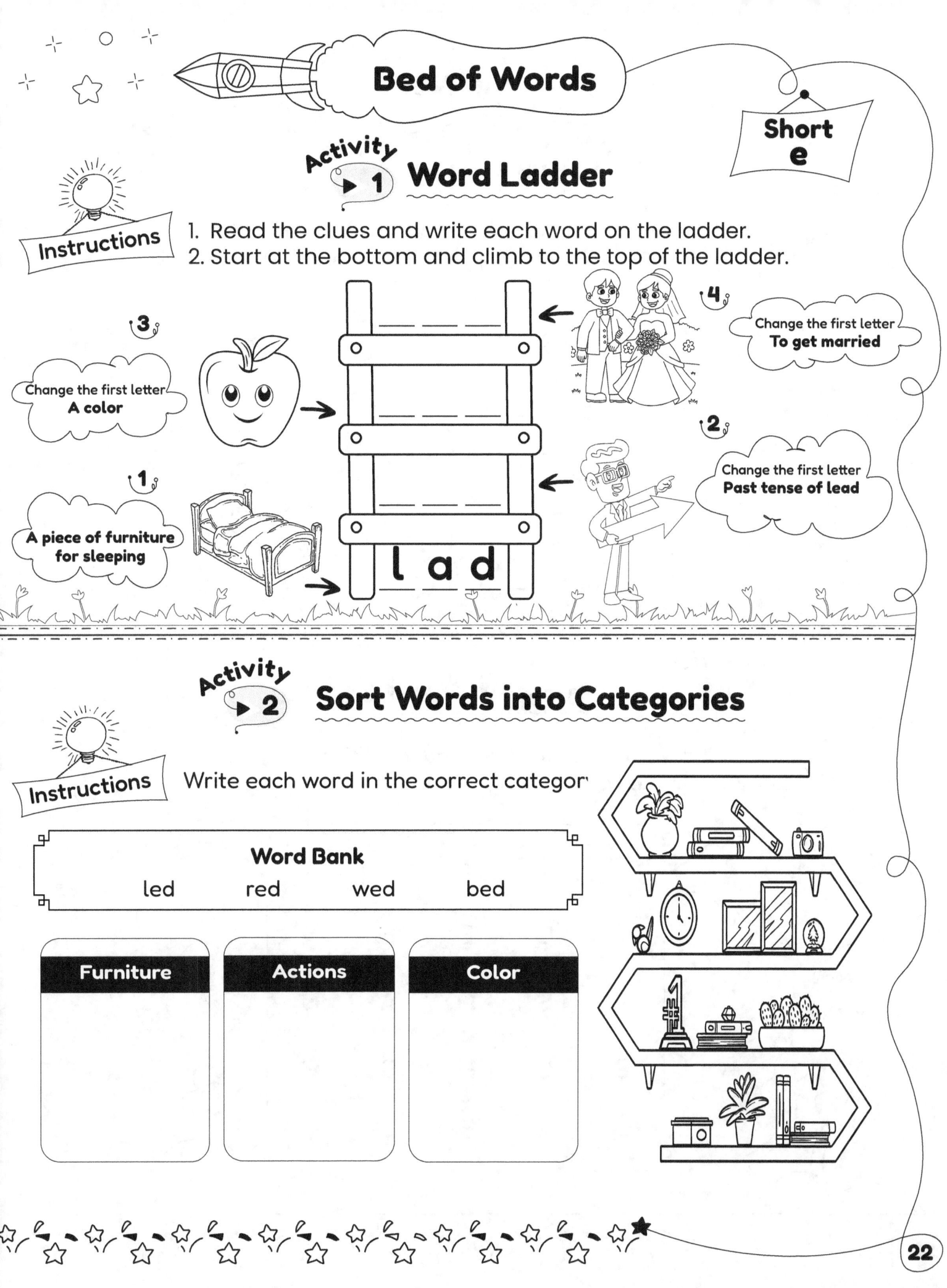

In the Net

Activity ▶ 1 Word Ladder

1. Read the clues and write each word on the ladder.
2. Start at the bottom and climb to the top of the ladder.

4 Change 'p' to 's'
To place something

3 Change 'b' to 'p'
Animal companion

2 Change 'n' to 'b'
To risk something

1 **Material for catching**

n e t

Activity ▶ 2 Simple Word Search

1. Find words from the word ladder within the grid.
2. Circle the words when you find them

C	I	T	T	V
T	C	E	E	N
E	S	D	A	N
B	C	N	S	H
H	A	P	E	T

Jet to Get Fun

Activity 1 — Word Ladder

Instructions

1. Read the clues and write each word on the ladder.
2. Start at the bottom and climb to the top of the ladder.

3 Change 'w' to 'm'
Saw someone you know

4 Change 'm' to 'g'
To receive something

1 **A fast airplane**

2 Change 'j' to 'w'
Covered with water

j e t

Activity 2 — Identify Consonants and Vowels

Instructions

1. Look at the words from the word ladder.
2. Circle the consonants in each word.
3. Underline the vowel in each word.

1) m e t

2) j e t

3) g e t

4) w e t

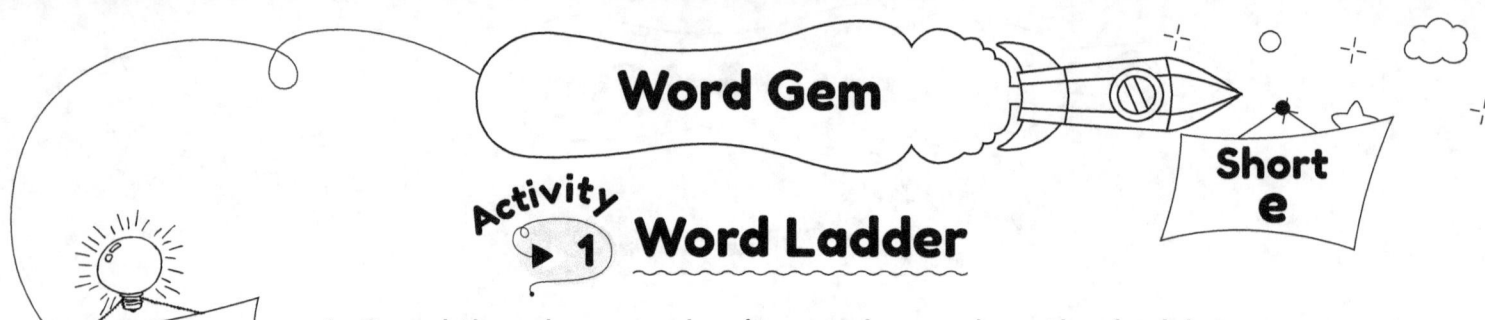

Word Gem

Activity ▸ 1 Word Ladder

Instructions

1. Read the clues and write each word on the ladder.
2. Start at the bottom and climb to the top of the ladder.

3. Change 'w' to 't' and 'b' to 'n'
The number after nine

1. A precious stone

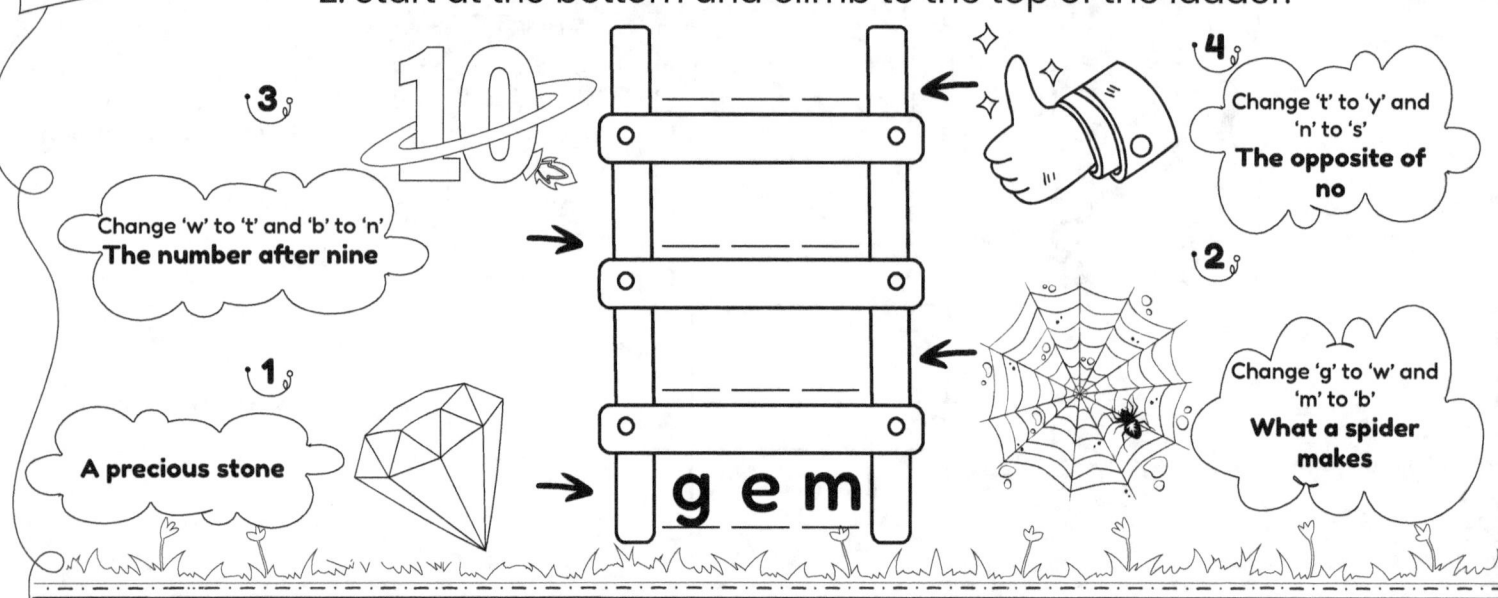

4. Change 't' to 'y' and 'n' to 's'
The opposite of no

2. Change 'g' to 'w' and 'm' to 'b'
What a spider makes

g e m

Activity ▸ 2 Circle the Short E Words

Instructions

Encircle all the words that have the short e sound.

Ben and His Pet Hen

Ben had a red pet hen. Every morning, he fed her a gem and some bread. One day, Ben's hen made a big web in the pen. Ben said, "Yes, that is a nice web, but hens don't make webs!"

Well Done

Activity 1 Word Ladder

Instructions

1. Read the clues and write each word on the ladder.
2. Start at the bottom and climb to the top of the ladder.

3 Change 'f' to 's'
To give something for money

4 Change 's' to 't'
To say something to someone.

2 Change 'w' to 'f'
What happens when you trip and go down.

1 A deep hole to get water.

w e l l

Activity 2 Color the Shell

Instructions

Color the shell that has words from the -ell word family.

bell

cat

yell

top

hop

fell

well

hop

dog

tell

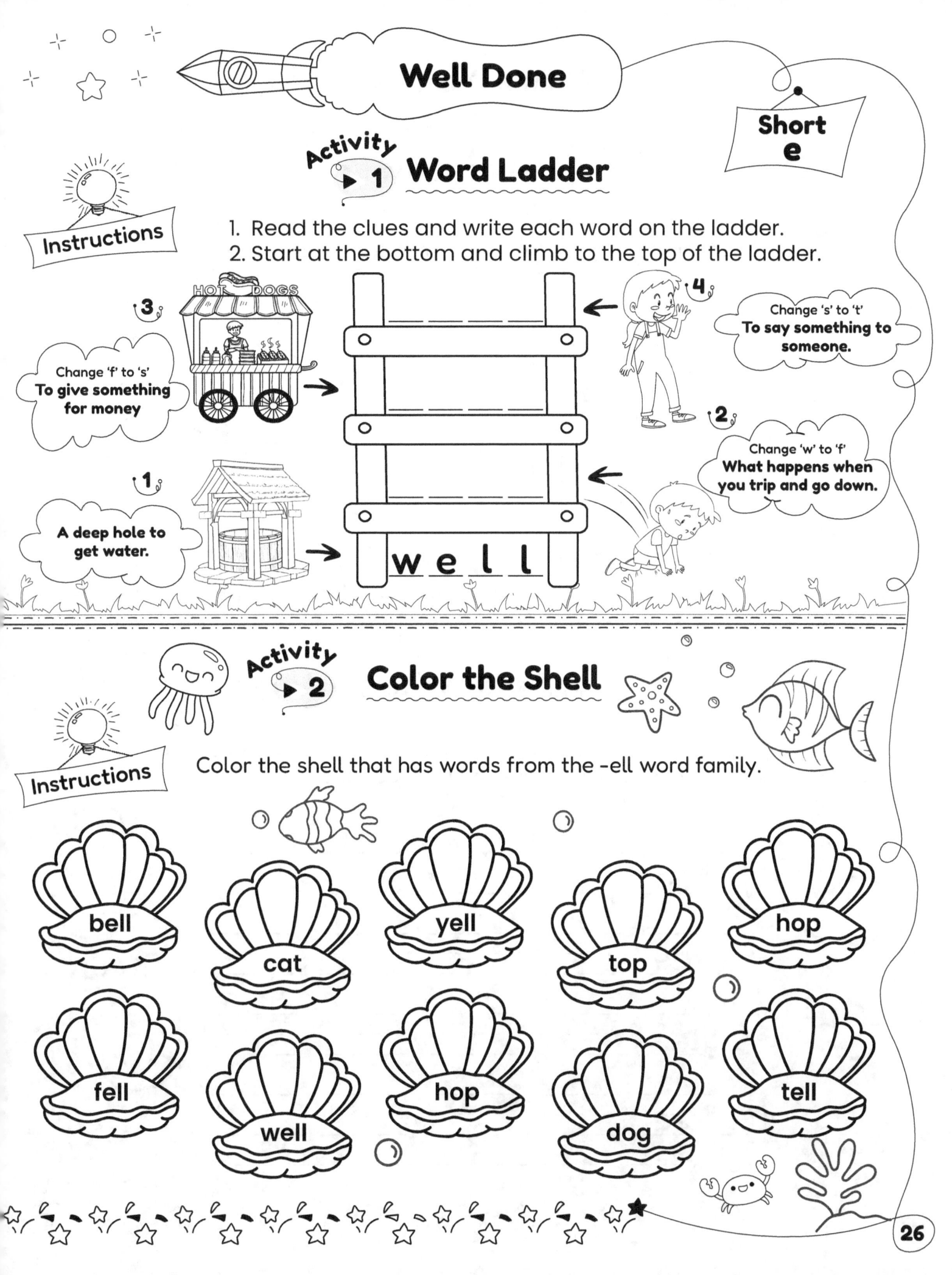

26

Climb the Tree

long e

Word Ladder

1. Read the clues and write each word on the ladder.
2. Start at the bottom and climb to the top of the ladder.

4 Change 'g' to 'f'
To run away quickly

3 Change 'fr' to 'gl'
A feeling of great happiness

2 Change 't' to 'f'
Not costing anything

1 **A tall plant with a trunk, branches, and leaves**

t r e e

Trace and Write the Words

1. Trace each word from the word ladder in the space provided.
2. Practice writing each word on your own.

1. flee
2. tree
3. glee
4. free

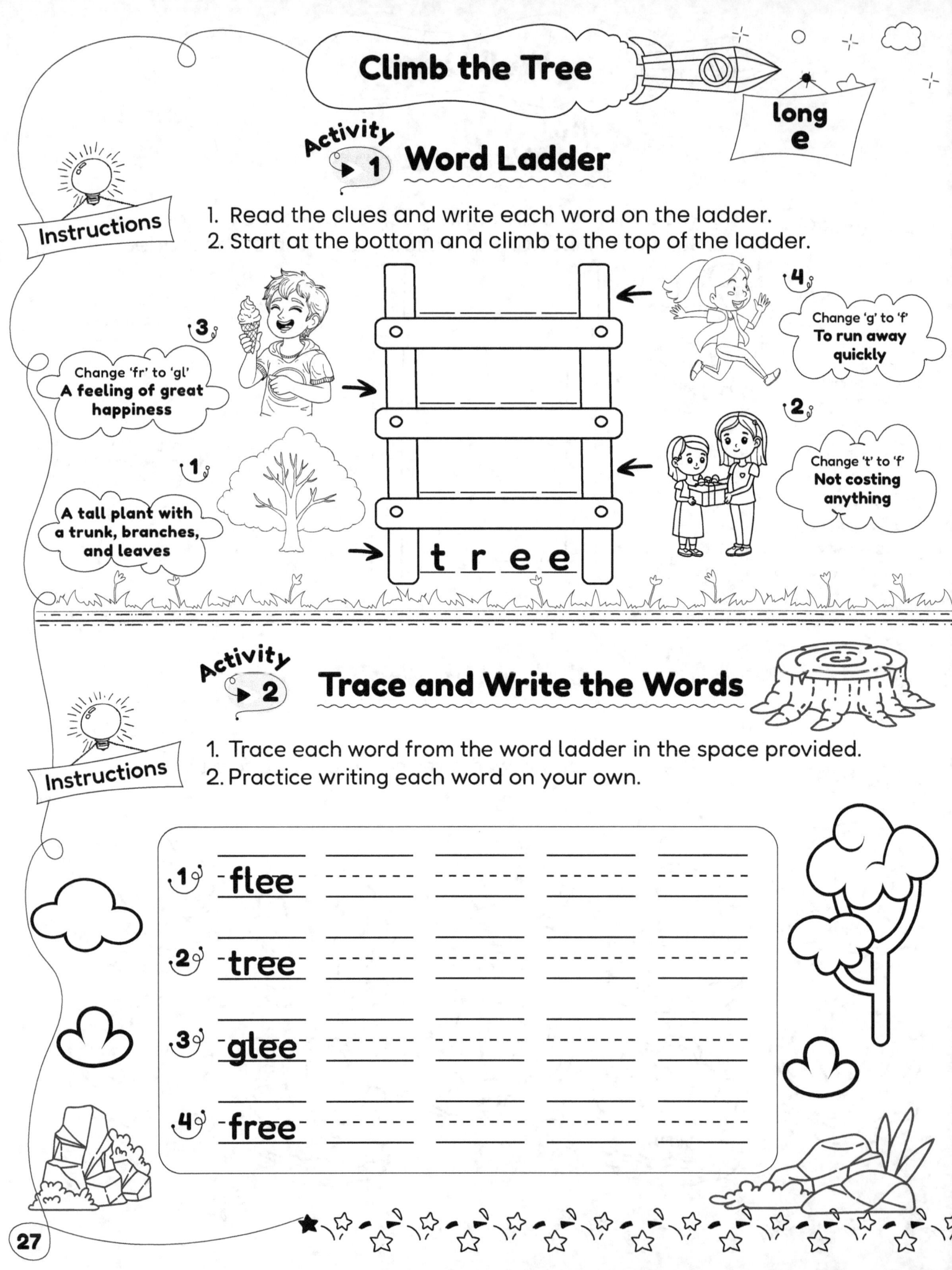

Sweet Feet Fun

long e

Activity 1 Word Ladder

Instructions
1. Read the clues and write each word on the ladder.
2. Start at the bottom and climb to the top of the ladder.

3 Change 'd' to 'n' and 'p' to 'd'
To require something

1 The part of your body you stand on.

4 Change 'n' to 'b' and 'd' to 'f'
Meat from a cow

2 Change f' to 'd' and 't' to 'p'
Far down or far in

f e e t

Activity 2 Sort Words into Categories

Instructions Write each word in the correct category.

Word Bank
pen
sweet
red
bet
feet
net
beef
need

Long 'e' Sound	Short 'e' sound

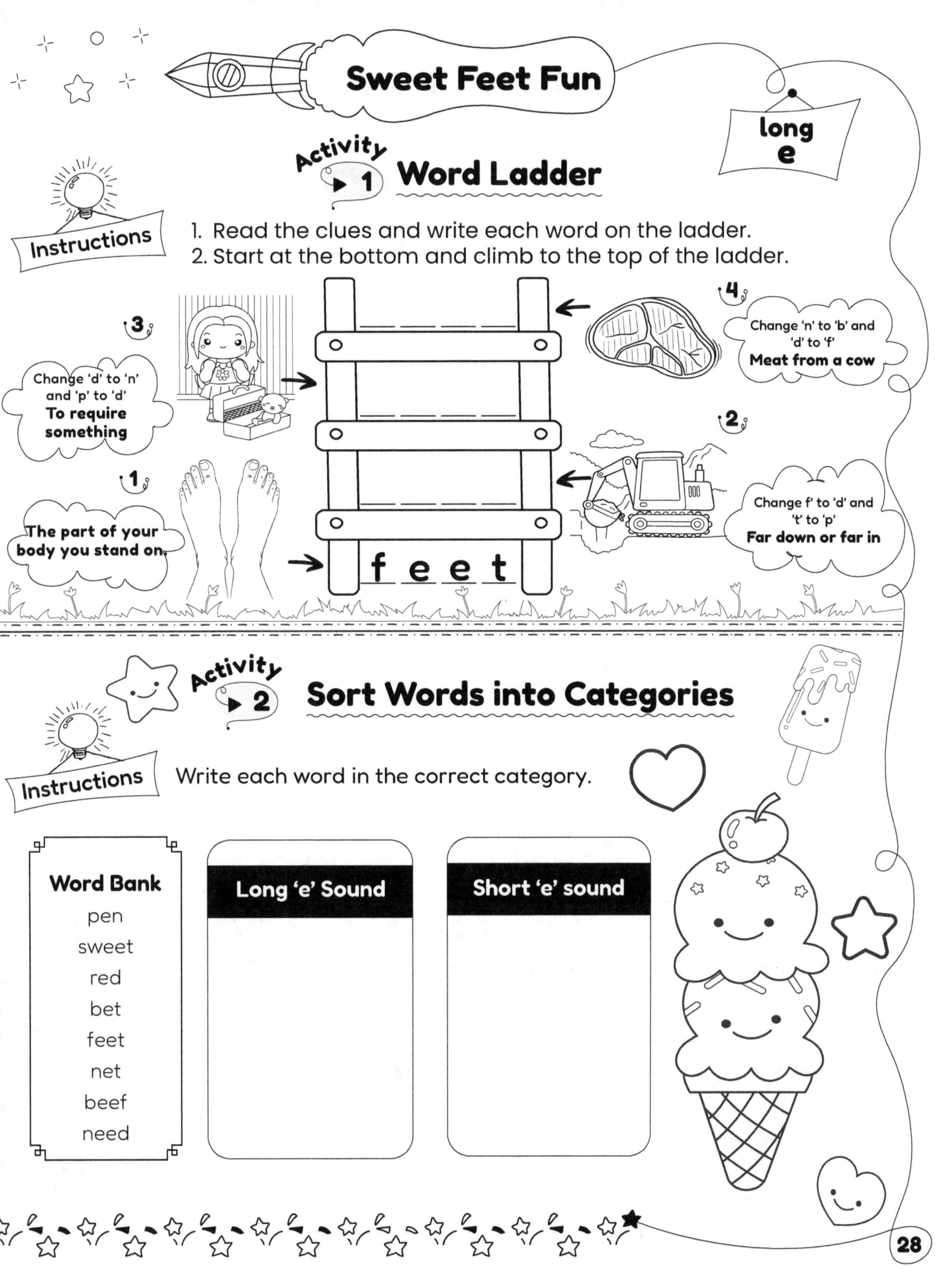

What's the Tea?

long e

Word Ladder

Instructions

1. Read the clues and write each word on the ladder.
2. Start at the bottom and climb to the top of the ladder.

3 Replace 'o' with 'h' **Something you wear on your head.**

4 Replace 'h' with 'b' **Something you hit a ball with.**

1 **What you do with food.**

2 Replace 'e' with 'o' at the beginning **A type of grain used in breakfast cereals**

e a t

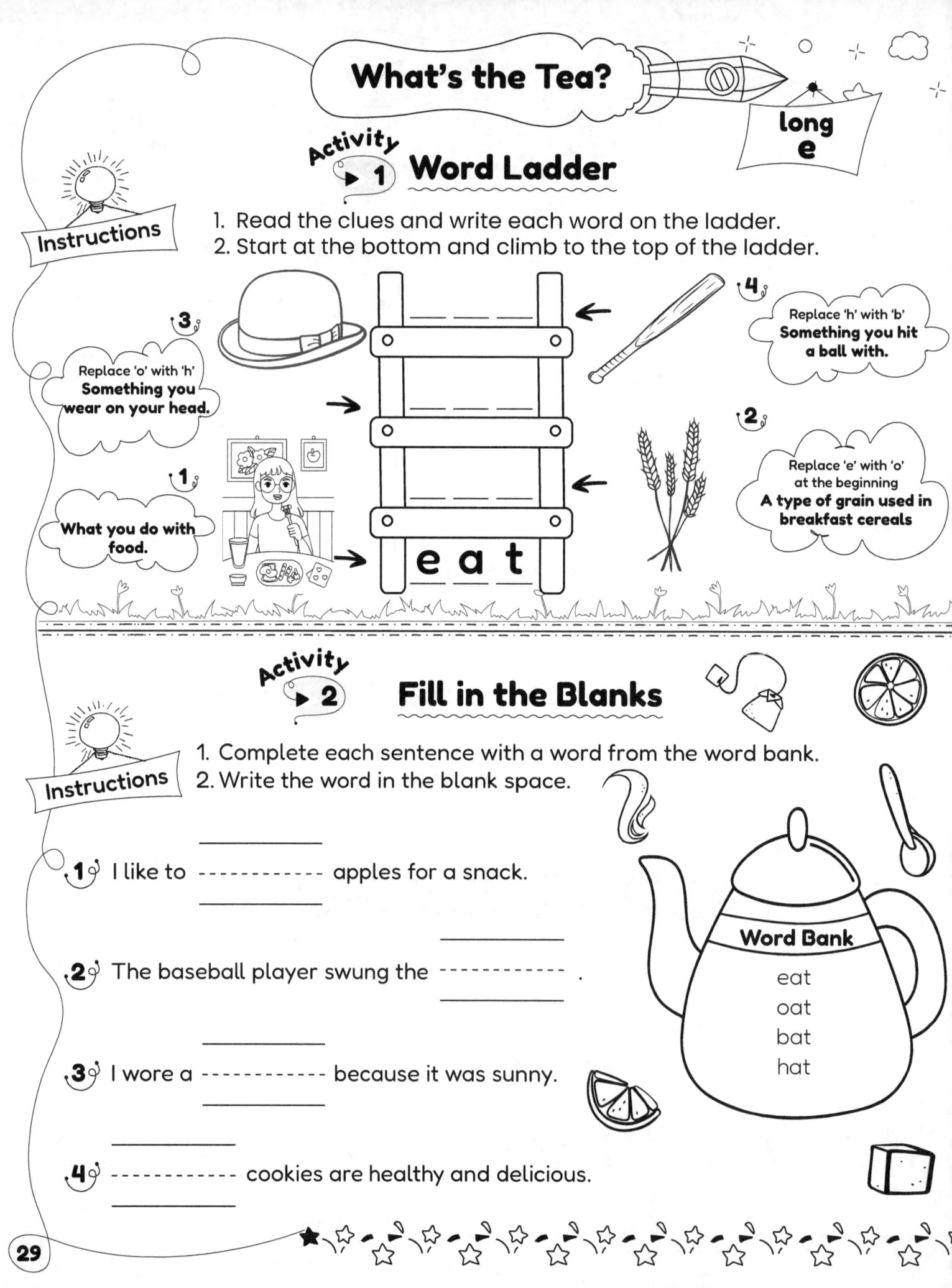

Activity ► 2 **Fill in the Blanks**

Instructions

1. Complete each sentence with a word from the word bank.
2. Write the word in the blank space.

1 I like to ----------- apples for a snack.

2 The baseball player swung the ----------- .

3 I wore a ----------- because it was sunny.

4 ----------- cookies are healthy and delicious.

Word Bank

eat
oat
bat
hat

29

Building with Kid

Short i

Activity 1 Word Ladder

Instructions

1. Read the clues and write each word on the ladder.
2. Start at the bottom and climb to the top of the ladder.

3 Change the first letter **To offer a price for something**

4 Change the first letter **To free someone or something from**

2 Change the first letter **A cover for a container**

1 A young goat or a child.

k i d

Activity 2 Match the Synonyms

Instructions

1. Match each word with its synonym.
2. Write the matching word next to each word from the choices.

1) kid ----------

2) lid ----------

3) bid ----------

4) rid ----------

cover

offer

remove

child

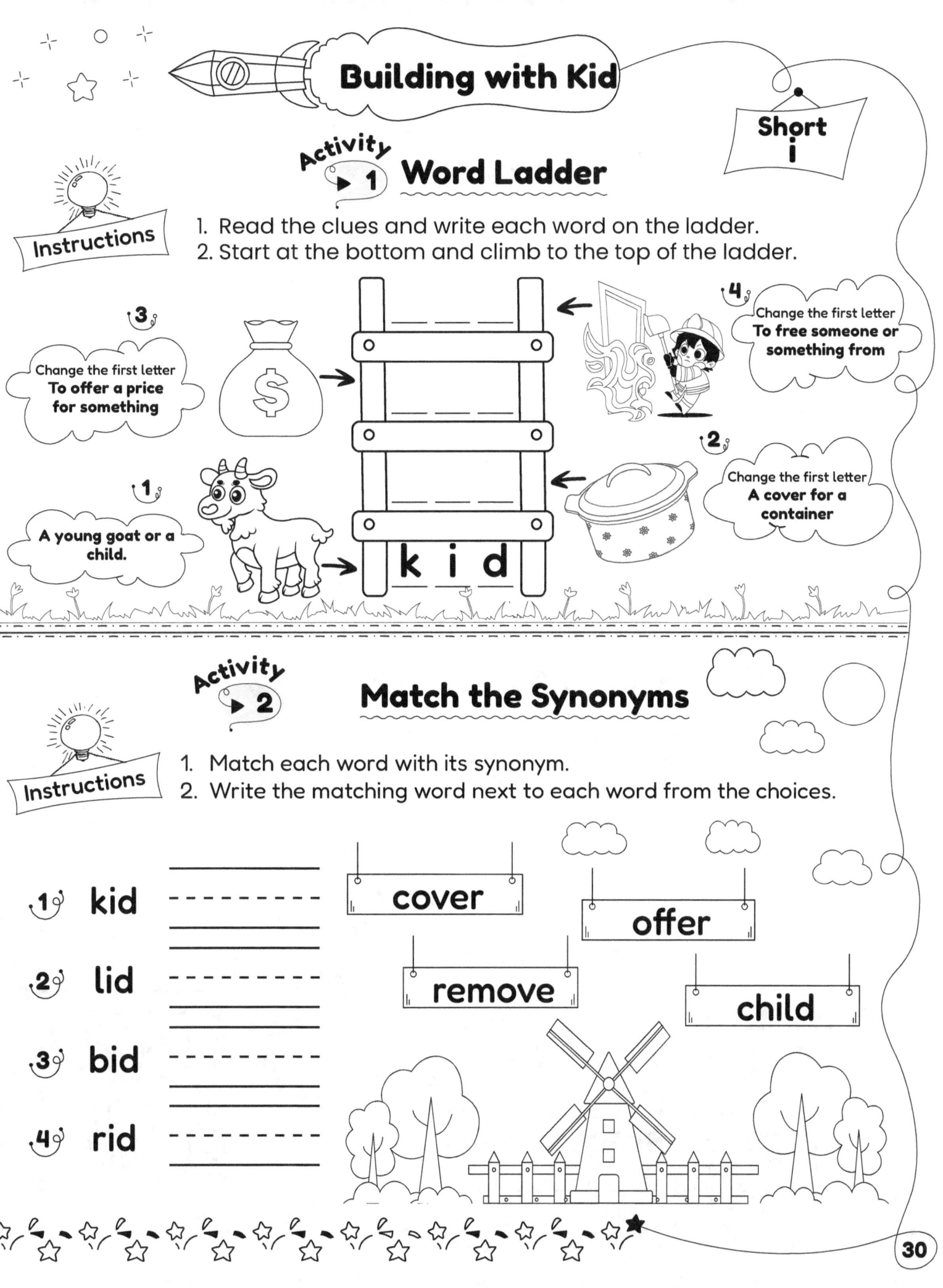

30

Tin Word Climb

Activity 1 Word Ladder

1. Read the clues and write each word on the ladder.
2. Start at the bottom and climb to the top of the ladder.

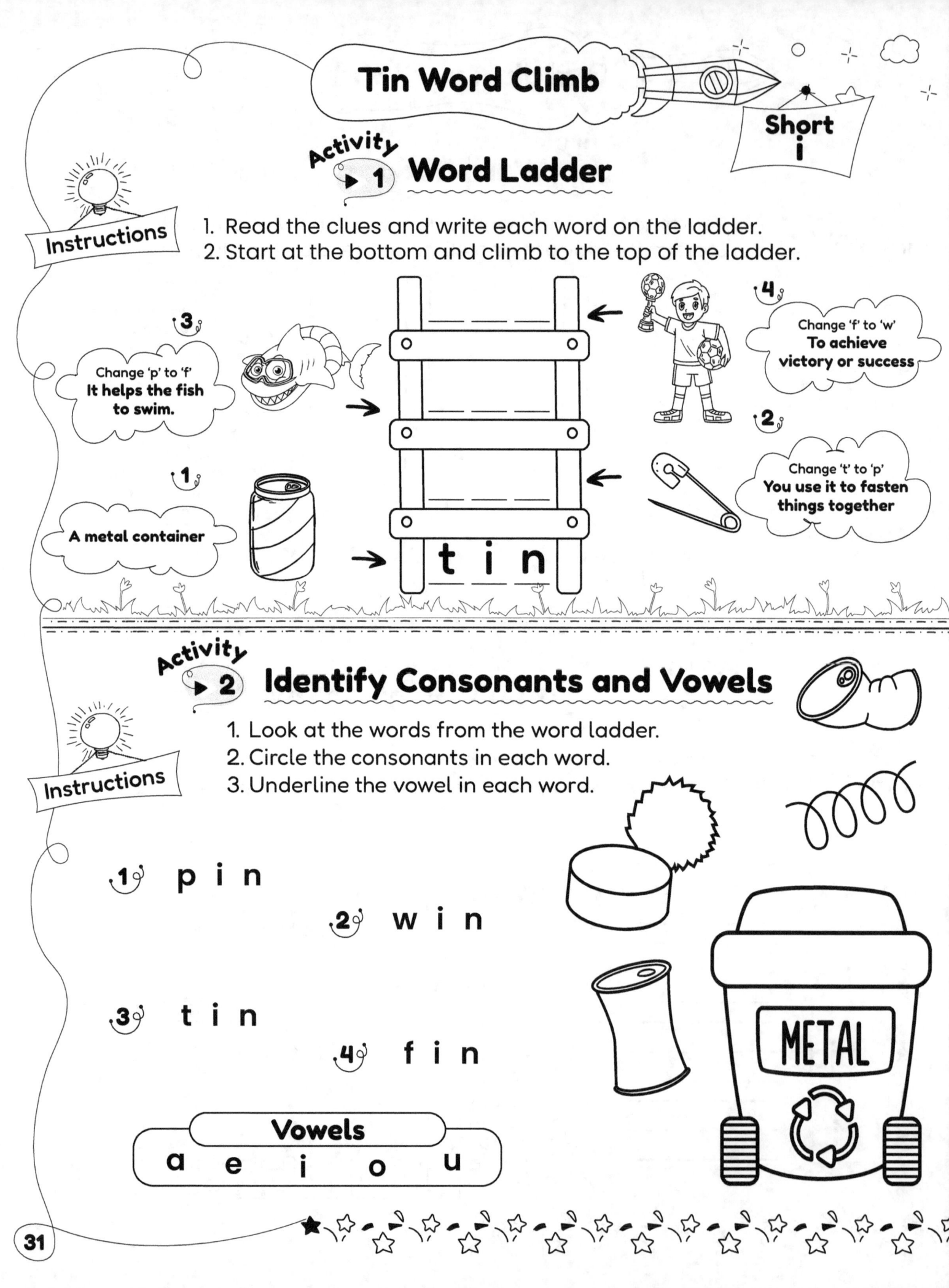

3 Change 'p' to 'f'
It helps the fish to swim.

4 Change 'f' to 'w'
To achieve victory or success

2 Change 't' to 'p'
You use it to fasten things together

1 A metal container

t i n

Activity 2 Identify Consonants and Vowels

1. Look at the words from the word ladder.
2. Circle the consonants in each word.
3. Underline the vowel in each word.

1) p i n
2) w i n
3) t i n
4) f i n

Vowels
a e i o u

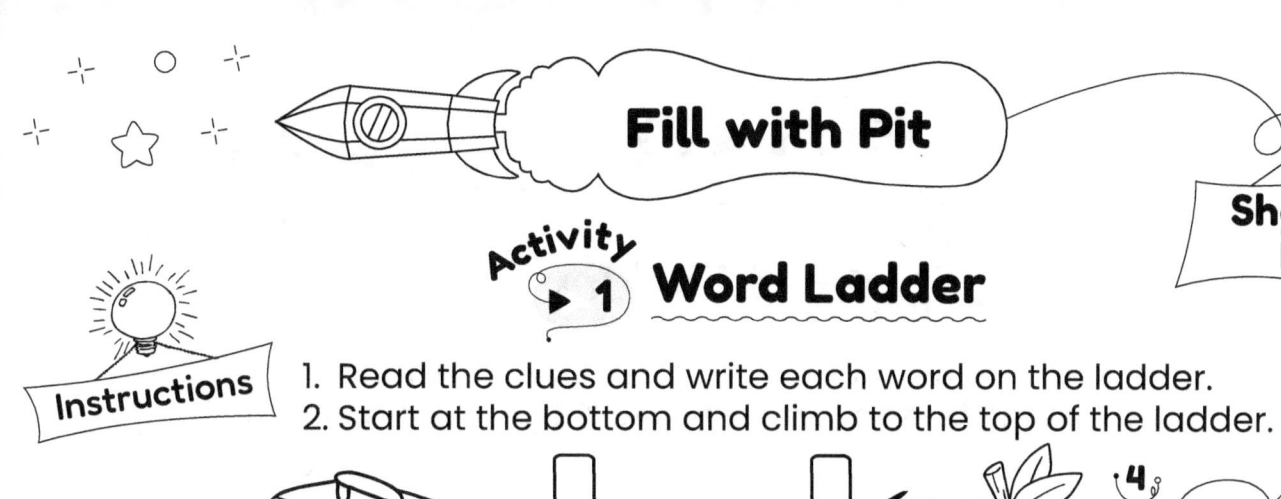

Fill with Pit

Activity 1 Word Ladder

Instructions
1. Read the clues and write each word on the ladder.
2. Start at the bottom and climb to the top of the ladder.

3 Change 'h' to 'k'
A set of tools or equipment

1 **A large hole in the ground**

4 Change 'k' to 'b'
To cut or crush with teeth

2 Change 'p' to 'h'
To strike something

p i t

Activity 2 Fill in the Blanks

Instructions
1. Complete each sentence with a word from the word bank.
2. Write the word in the blank space.

1 He will ----------- the ball with the bat.

2 The road has a large ----------- at the center.

3 He ----------- into the apple.

4 The first aid ----------- has bandages.

Find the Zip

Activity 1 Word Ladder

Instructions

1. Read the clues and write each word on the ladder.
2. Start at the bottom and climb to the top of the ladder.

4. Change the first letter
To drink something slowly

3. Change the first letter
The pointed end of something

2. Change the first letter
The edge of the mouth

1. **To fasten something with a zipper**

z i p

Activity 2 Practice High-Frequency Words

Instructions

1. Look at each flashcard with a sight word.
2. Read the word aloud.
3. Practice writing the word in the space provided.

| lip | zip | sip | tip |

Fix the Tap

Activity 1 Word Ladder

Instructions

1. Read the clues and write each word on the ladder.
2. Start at the bottom and climb to the top of the ladder.

3 Change 'm' to 's'
The number after five

1 To repair something

4 Change 's' to 'n'
To stop something from happening

2 Change 'f' to 'm'
To combine things together

f   i   x

Activity 2 Match Antonyms and Synonyms

Instructions

1. Match each word with its antonym or synonym.
2. Write the matching word next to each word from the choices.

1 fix (antonym) _ _ _ _ _ _ _ _

2 mix (synonym) _ _ _ _ _ _ _ _

3 six (synonym) _ _ _ _ _ _ _ _

4 nix (antonym) _ _ _ _ _ _ _ _

Choices
allow
blend
half a dozen
break

Follow the Hill

Activity 1 Word Ladder

1. Read the clues and write each word on the ladder.
2. Start at the bottom and climb to the top of the ladder.

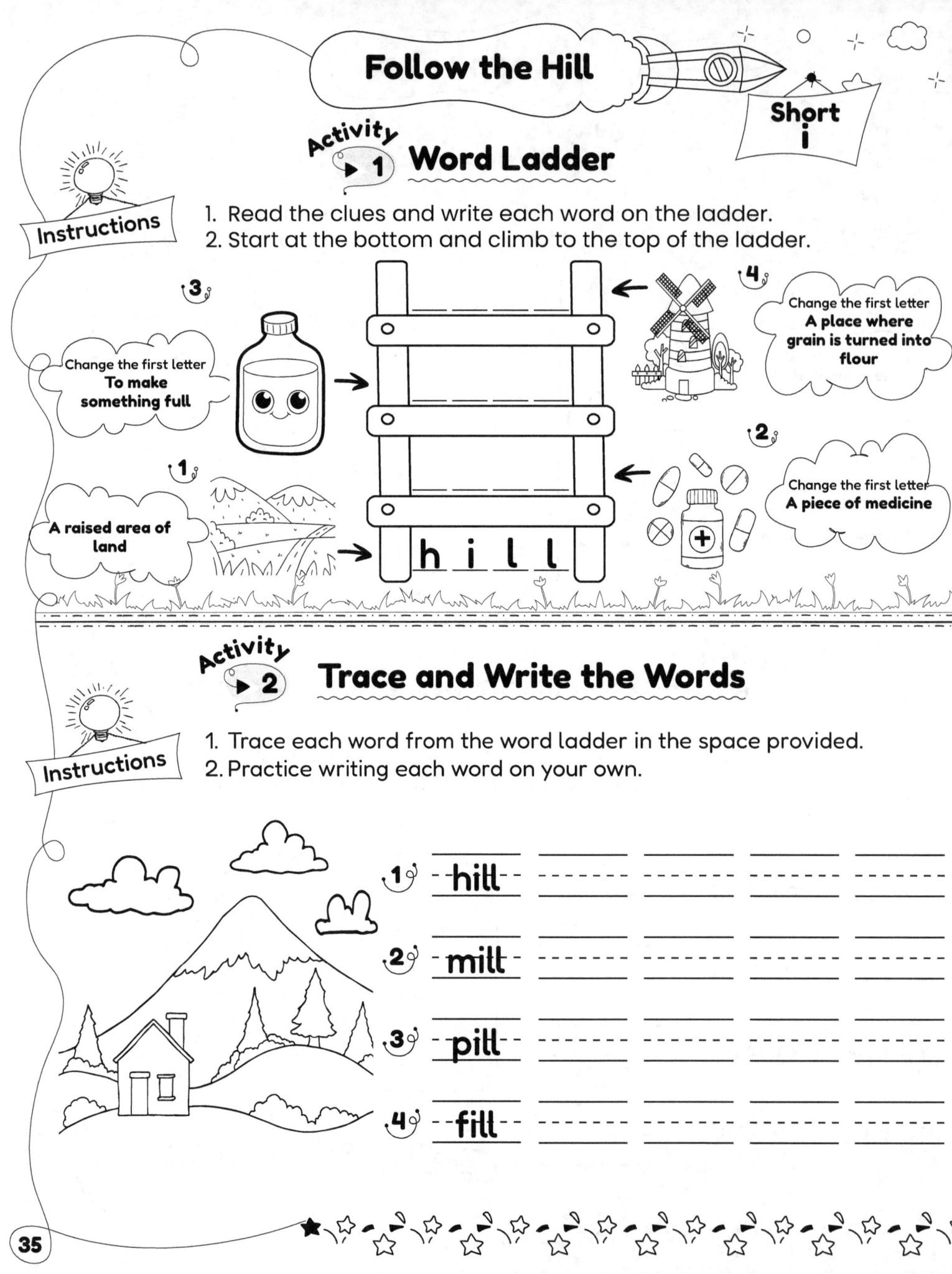

3 Change the first letter
To make something full

4 Change the first letter
A place where grain is turned into flour

1 A raised area of land

2 Change the first letter
A piece of medicine

h i l l

Activity 2 Trace and Write the Words

1. Trace each word from the word ladder in the space provided.
2. Practice writing each word on your own.

1. hill
2. mill
3. pill
4. fill

35

Fun with Wig

Activity ➤ 1 Word Ladder

Instructions

1. Read the clues and write each word on the ladder.
2. Start at the bottom and climb to the top of the ladder.

3
Change 'r' to 'b'
Cloth worn while eating to keep clothes clean

4
Change 'b' to 'n'
A container for storing things

1
Something you wear on your head

2
Change 'w' and 'g' to 'r' and 'b'
A bonethat protects your chest

w i g

Activity ➤ 2 Alphabetical Order Exercises

Instructions

1. Look at the list of words from the word ladder.
2. Write the words in alphabetical order in the spaces provided.

1. _____
2. _____
3. _____
4. _____

Word Bank
rib
wig
bin
bib

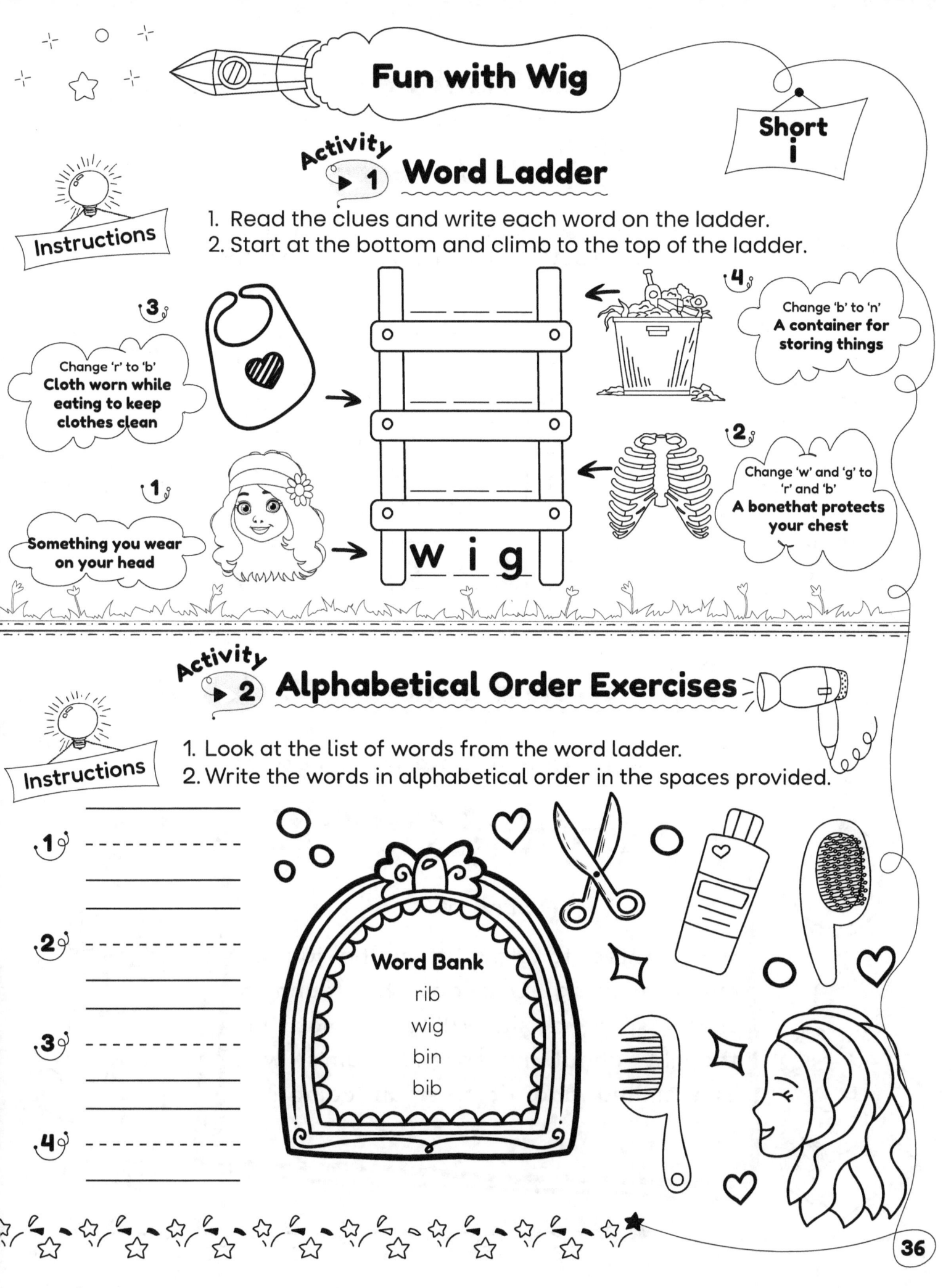

Get Fit with Wit

Short i

Activity 1 — Word Ladder

Instructions

1. Read the clues and write each word on the ladder.
2. Start at the bottom and climb to the top of the ladder.

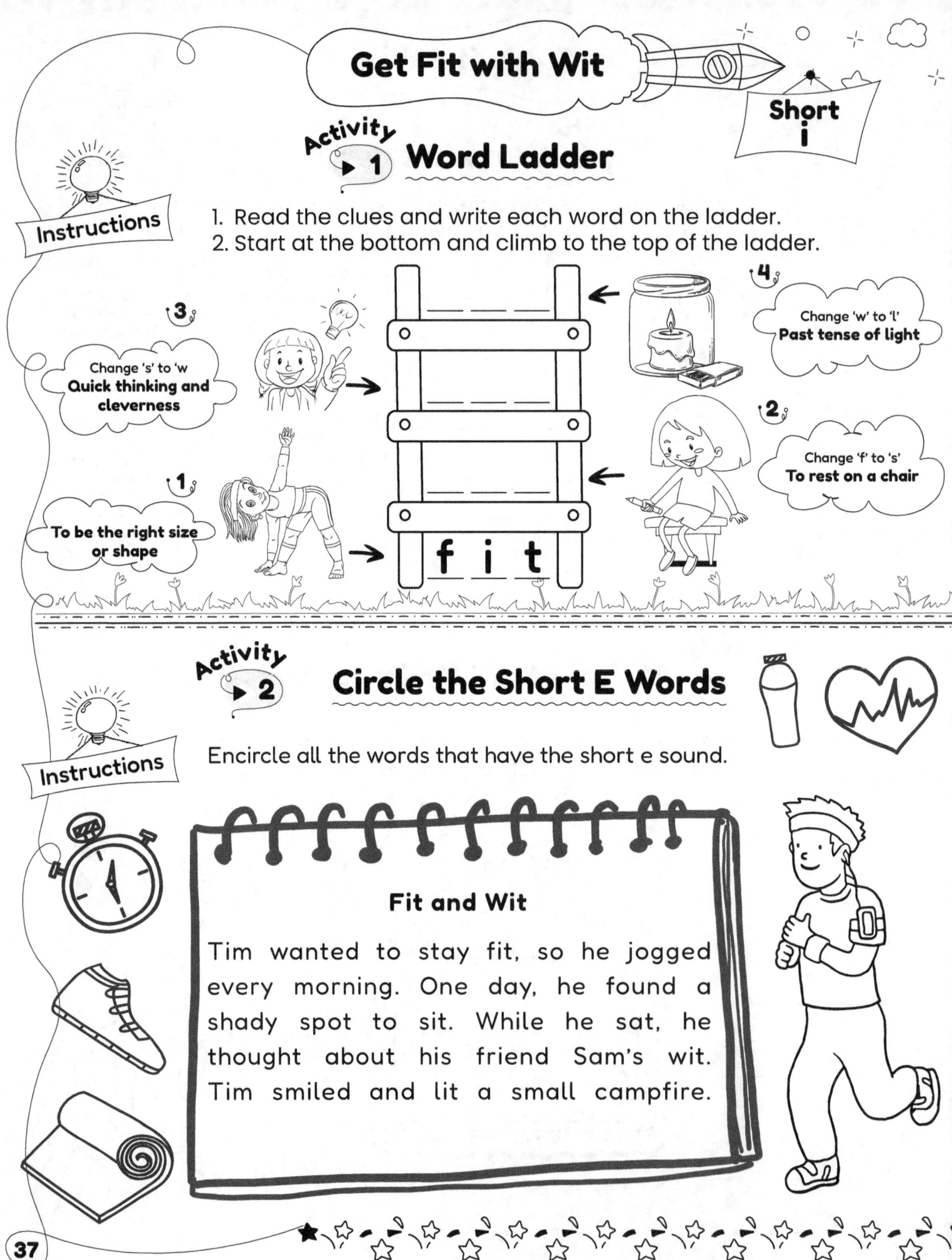

4 Change 'w' to 'l'
Past tense of light

3 Change 's' to 'w'
Quick thinking and cleverness

2 Change 'f' to 's'
To rest on a chair

1 To be the right size or shape

f i t

Activity 2 — Circle the Short E Words

Instructions

Encircle all the words that have the short e sound.

Fit and Wit

Tim wanted to stay fit, so he jogged every morning. One day, he found a shady spot to sit. While he sat, he thought about his friend Sam's wit. Tim smiled and lit a small campfire.

Pack for a Trip

Activity 1 — Word Ladder

1. Read the clues and write each word on the ladder.
2. Start at the bottom and climb to the top of the ladder.

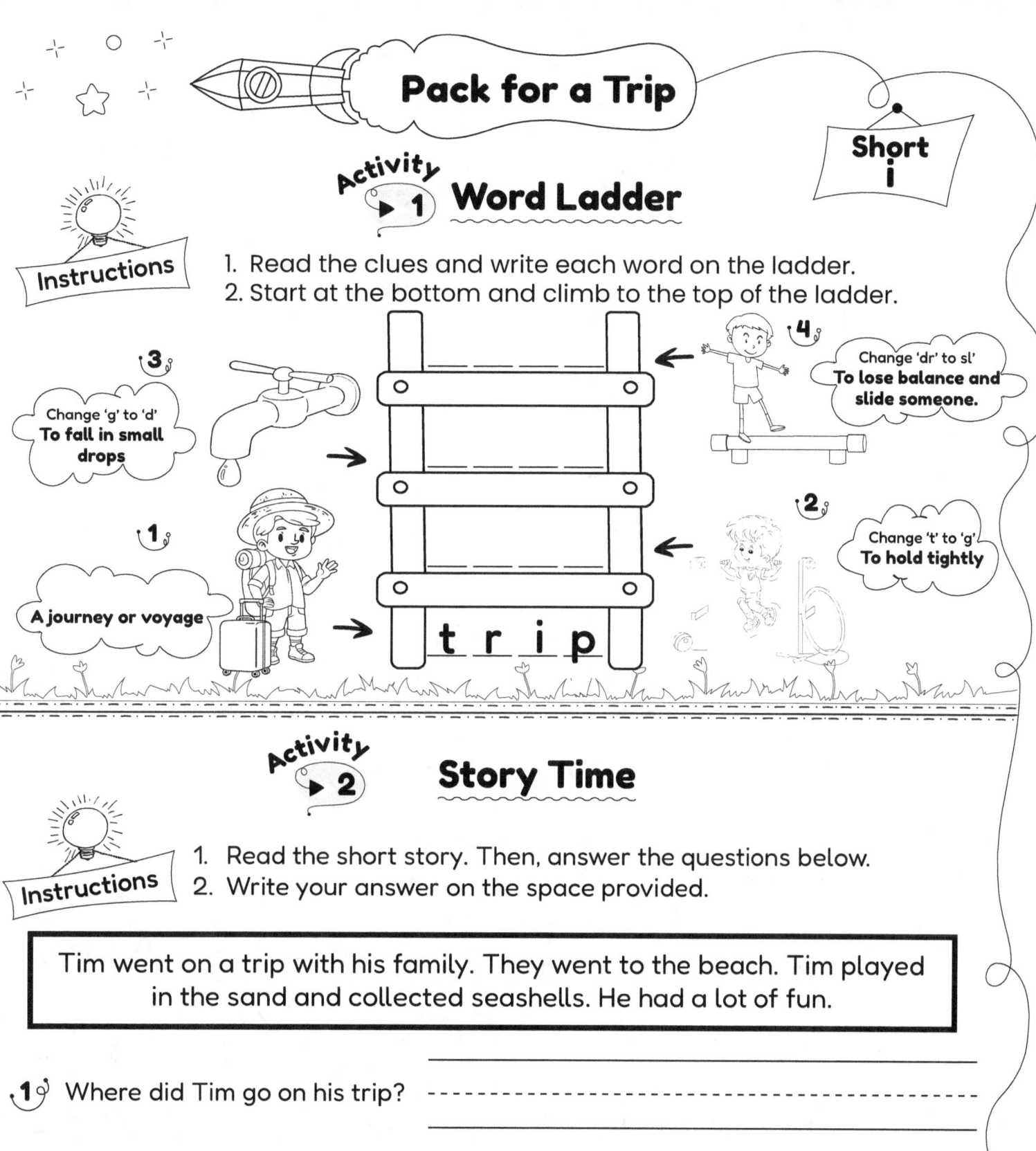

3 Change 'g' to 'd'
To fall in small drops

1 A journey or voyage

4 Change 'dr' to 'sl'
To lose balance and slide someone.

2 Change 't' to 'g'
To hold tightly

t r i p

Activity 2 — Story Time

1. Read the short story. Then, answer the questions below.
2. Write your answer on the space provided.

Tim went on a trip with his family. They went to the beach. Tim played in the sand and collected seashells. He had a lot of fun.

1 Where did Tim go on his trip?

2 What did Tim play with?

3 What did Tim collect?

Play with Pig

Activity ► 1 Word Ladder

1. Read the clues and write each word on the ladder.
2. Start at the bottom and climb to the top of the ladder.

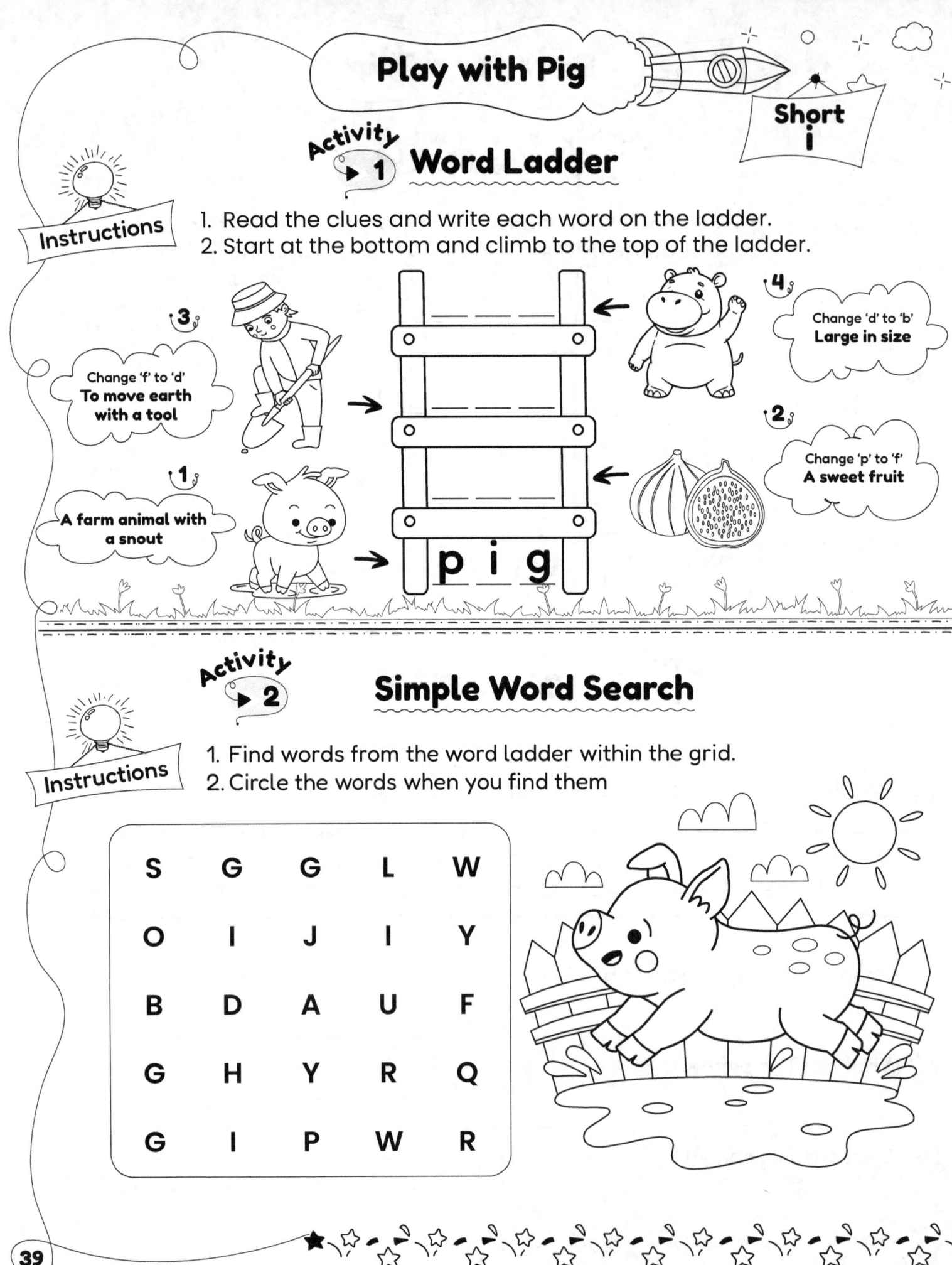

3. Change 'f' to 'd'
To move earth with a tool

4. Change 'd' to 'b'
Large in size

2. Change 'p' to 'f'
A sweet fruit

1. A farm animal with a snout

p i g

Activity ► 2 Simple Word Search

1. Find words from the word ladder within the grid.
2. Circle the words when you find them

S	G	G	L	W
O	I	J	I	Y
B	D	A	U	F
G	H	Y	R	Q
G	I	P	W	R

Build with Rod

Activity 1 — Word Ladder

Instructions
1. Read the clues and write each word on the ladder.
2. Start at the bottom and climb to the top of the ladder.

3. Change the first letter
Short for body

4. Change the first letter
To move your head up and down

2. Change the first letter
A deity

1. A thin, straight bar

r o d

Activity 2 — Decode the Secret Words

Instructions
1. Use the key (a=1, b=2, etc.) to decode each number into a letter.
2. Write the decoded word in the space provided.

a	b	c	d	e	f	g	h	i	j	k	l	m	n	o	p	q	r	s	t	u	v	w	x	y	z
1	2	3	4	5	6	7	8	9	10	11	12	13	14	15	16	17	18	19	20	21	22	23	24	25	26

1. **7-15-4:** A special being people worship. _____

2. **14-15-4:** To move your head up and down. _____

3. **18-15-4:** A long, slender stick. _____

4. **2-15-4:** Another word for body. _____

Build with Top

Activity 1 — Word Ladder

Instructions

1. Read the clues and write each word on the ladder.
2. Start at the bottom and climb to the top of the ladder.

4 Replace 'm' with 'c'
Another word for a police officer

3 Replace 'p' with 'm'
A tool for cleaning floors

2 Replace 't' with 'p'
A sudden burst or sound

1 **The highest part of something**

t o p

Activity 2 — Rhyming Words Activity

Instructions

Draw a picture of your favorite word that rhymes with 'top'.

top

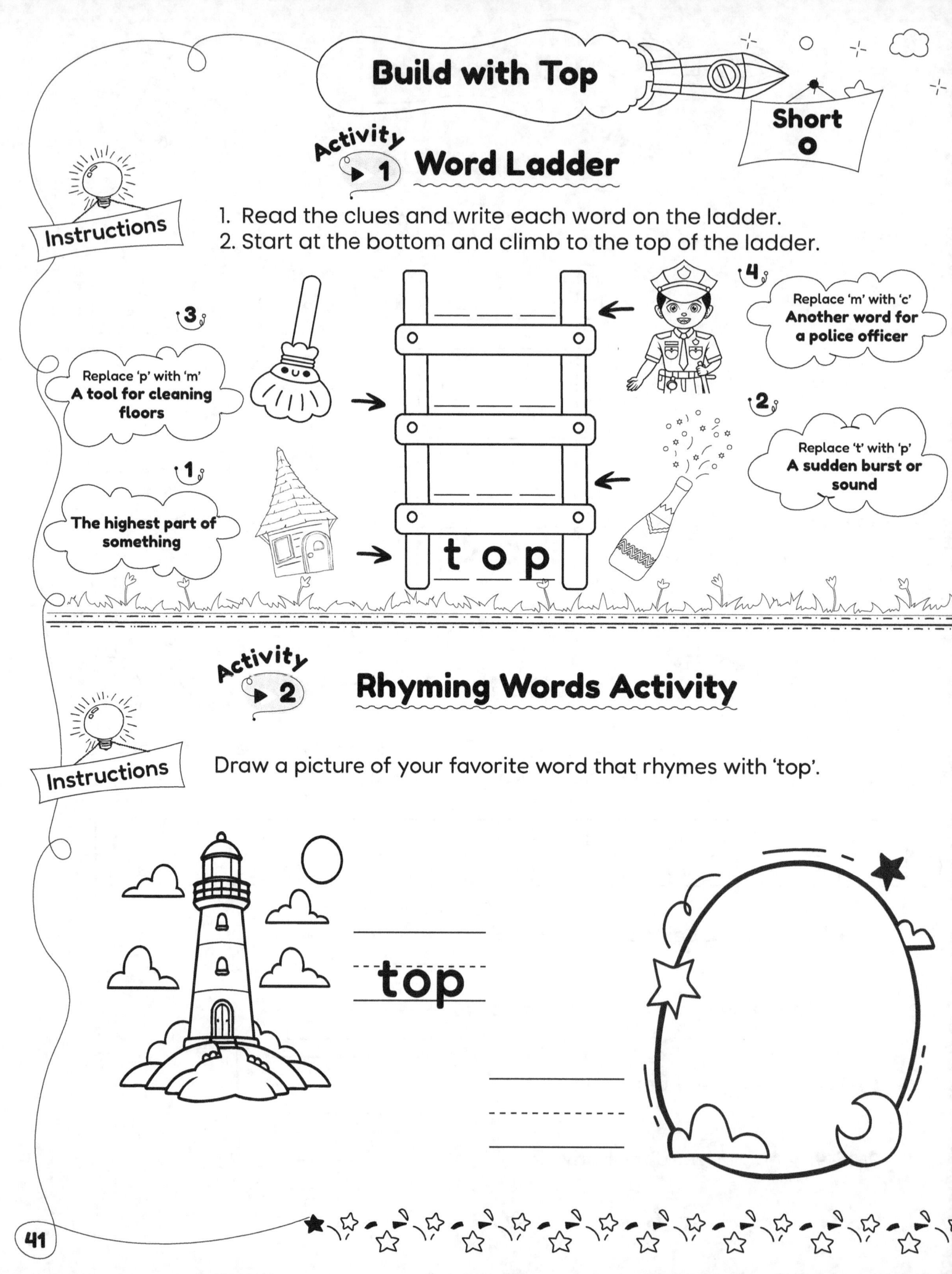

41

Dog's World

Activity 1 — Word Ladder

Instructions

1. Read the clues and write each word on the ladder.
2. Start at the bottom and climb to the top of the ladder.

3. Change the first letter
A thick cloud near the ground

4. Change the first letter
Another word for pig

1. **An animal that barks**

2. Change the first letter
A big piece of wood

d o g

Activity 2 — Fill in the Blanks

Instructions

1. Complete each sentence with a word from the word bank.
2. Write the word in the blank space.

1. The _____ barks when it sees a stranger.

2. The _____ made it hard to see the road.

3. A _____ is cut from a tree.

4. The farmer keeps a _____ in the barn.

Word Bank
hog
fog
log
dog

42

Jump on the Cob

Activity 1 — Word Ladder

1. Read the clues and write each word on the ladder.
2. Start at the bottom and climb to the top of the ladder.

4 Change 'r' to 's'
To cry noisily

3 Change 'j' to 'r'
To steal from someone

2 Change 'c' to 'j'
Work you do for money

1 The central part of corn

c o b

Activity 2 — Match the Synonyms

1. Match each word with its synonym.
2. Write the matching word next to each word from the choices.

1 cob — — — — —

2 job — — — — —

3 rob — — — — —

4 sob — — — — —

steal

core

cry

work

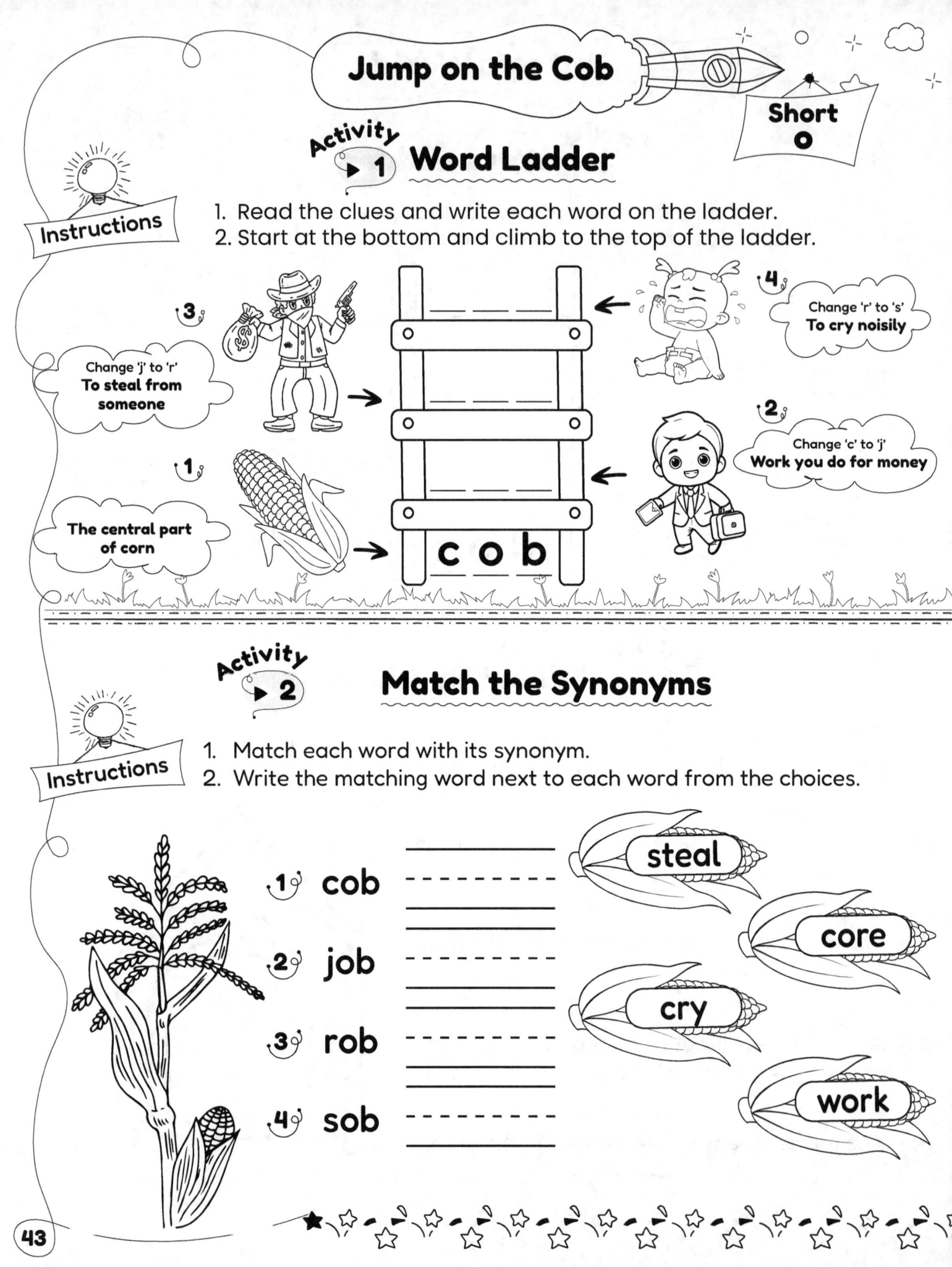

Magic in the Pot

Activity ▶ 1 Word Ladder

Instructions

1. Read the clues and write each word on the ladder.
2. Start at the bottom and climb to the top of the ladder.

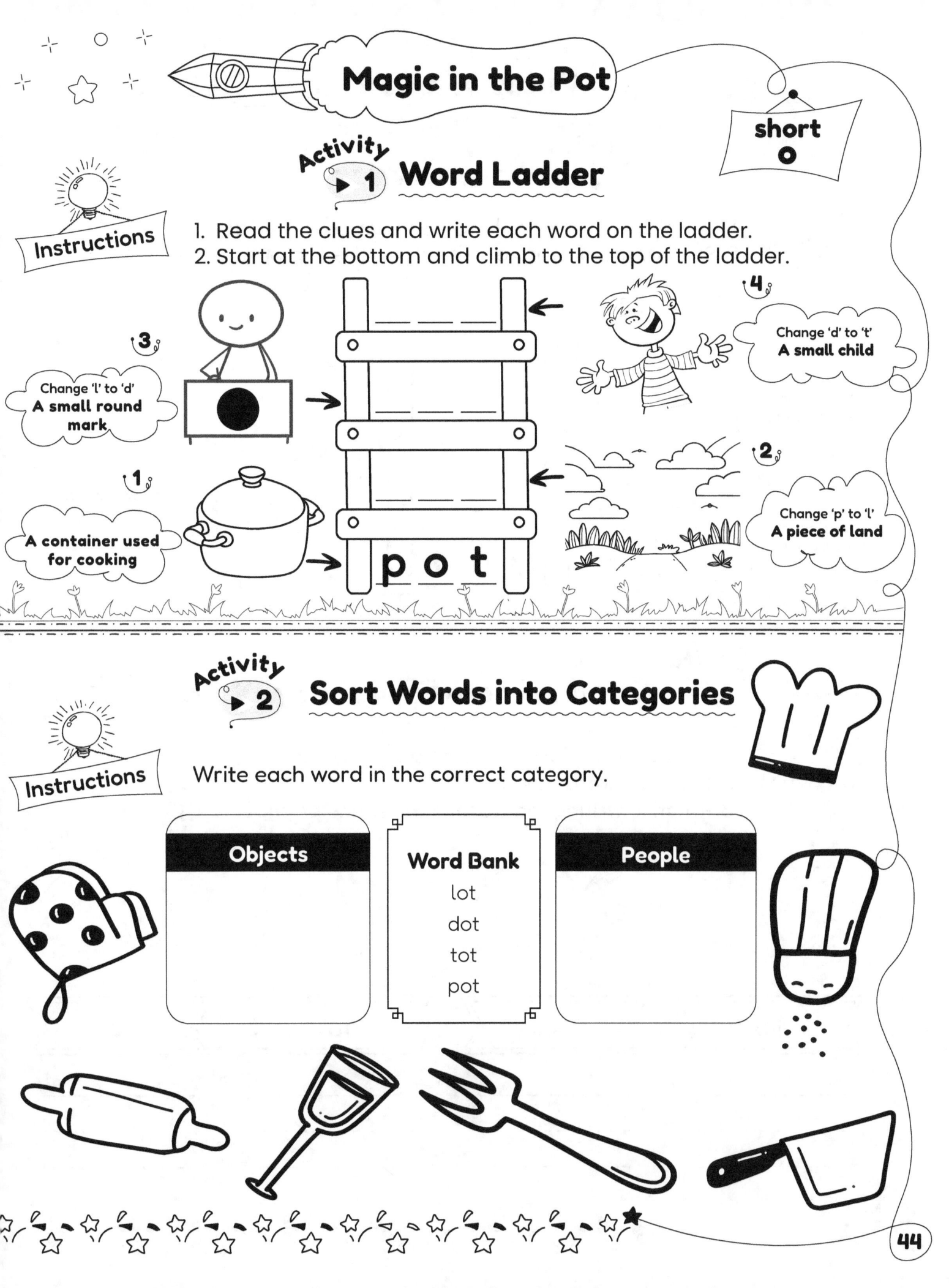

3 Change 'l' to 'd'
A small round mark

1 A container used for cooking

4 Change 'd' to 't'
A small child

2 Change 'p' to 'l'
A piece of land

p o t

Activity ▶ 2 Sort Words into Categories

Instructions

Write each word in the correct category.

Objects	Word Bank	People
	lot	
	dot	
	tot	
	pot	

Put It in a Box

Activity 1 Word Ladder

Instructions
1. Read the clues and write each word on the ladder.
2. Start at the bottom and climb to the top of the ladder.

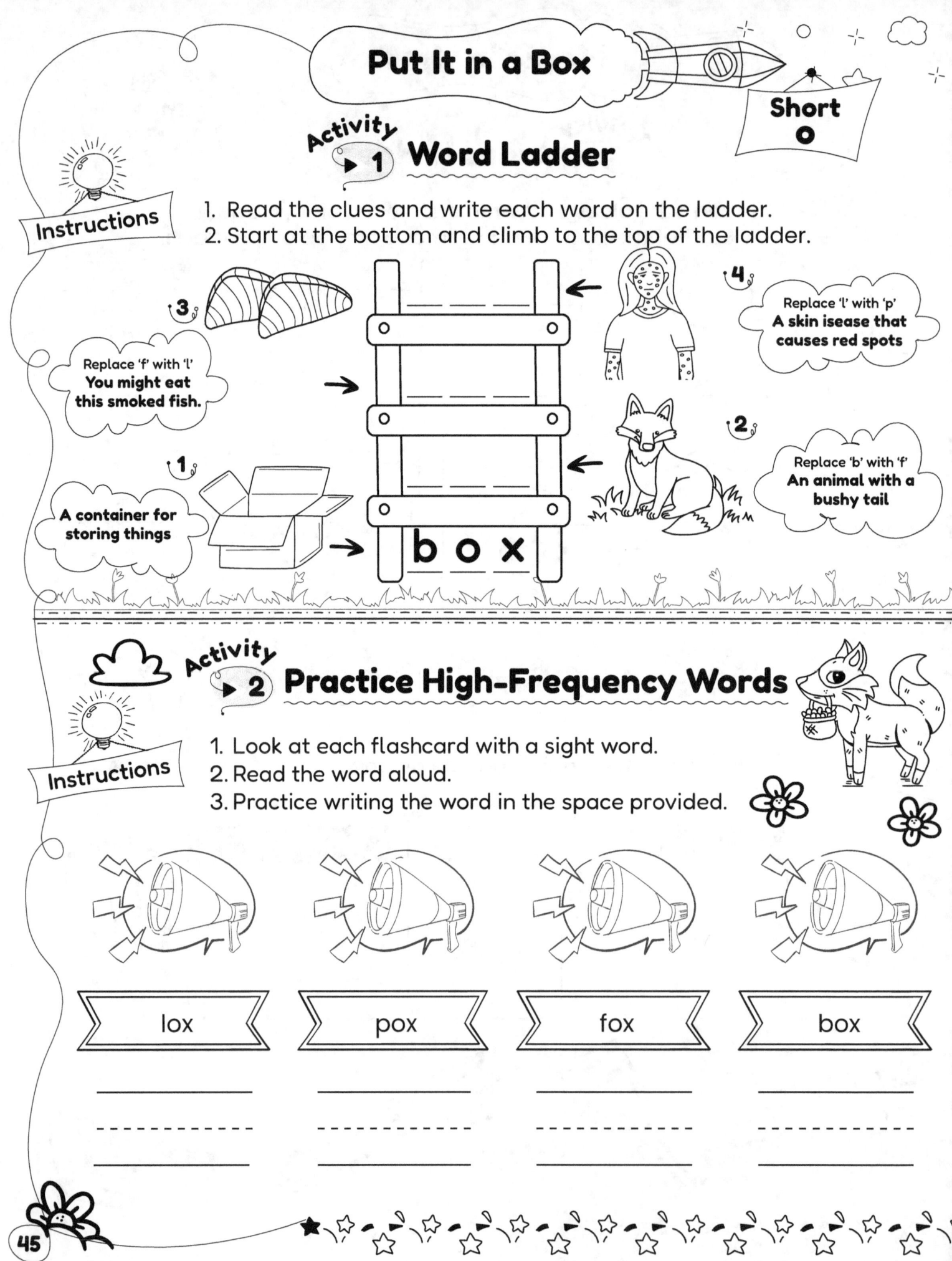

3 Replace 'f' with 'l'
You might eat this smoked fish.

4 Replace 'l' with 'p'
A skin isease that causes red spots

1 A container for storing things

2 Replace 'b' with 'f'
An animal with a bushy tail

b o x

Activity 2 Practice High-Frequency Words

Instructions
1. Look at each flashcard with a sight word.
2. Read the word aloud.
3. Practice writing the word in the space provided.

| lox | pox | fox | box |

Jot It While It's Hot!

short o

Activity 1 — Word Ladder

Instructions

1. Read the clues and write each word on the ladder.
2. Start at the bottom and climb to the top of the ladder.

3. Change 'r' to 'j'
To write something quickly

4. Change 'j' to 'n'
Makes a word or phrase negative.

1. **Having a high temperature.**

2. Change 'h' to 'r'
To decay or decompose.

h o t

Activity 2 — Trace and Write the Words

Instructions

1. Trace each word from the word ladder in the space provided.
2. Practice writing each word on your own.

1. hot
2. rot
3. jot
4. not

46

Who's the Boss?

Activity 1 Word Ladder

Instructions

1. Read the clues and write each word on the ladder.
2. Start at the bottom and climb to the top of the ladder.

4. Change 'm' to 't'
To throw gently.

3. Change 'l' to 'm'
A small green plant on wet surfaces.

2. Change 'b' to 'l'
When you don't have something anymore.

1. **A person in charge at work.**

b o s s

Activity 2 Alphabetical Order Exercises

Instructions

1. Look at the list of words from the word ladder.
2. Write the words in alphabetical order in the spaces provided.

1. _ _ _ _ _ _ _ _ 2. _ _ _ _ _ _ _ _ 3. _ _ _ _ _ _ _ _ 4. _ _ _ _ _ _ _ _

Word Bank
boss
moss
toss
loss

Go with Bow

long o

Activity 1 **Word Ladder**

Instructions

1. Read the clues and write each word on the ladder.
2. Start at the bottom and climb to the top of the ladder.

3 Replace 'l' with 'r'
A line of things or people

1 A curved weapon used for shooting arrows.

4 Replace 'r' with 'm'
To cut grass

2 Replace 'b' with 'l'
Not high

b o w

Activity 2 **Identify Consonants and Vowels**

LOVE

Instructions

1. Look at the words from the word ladder.
2. Circle the consonants in each word.
3. Underline the vowel in each word.

1 b o w   **2** l o w   **3** r o w   **4** m o w

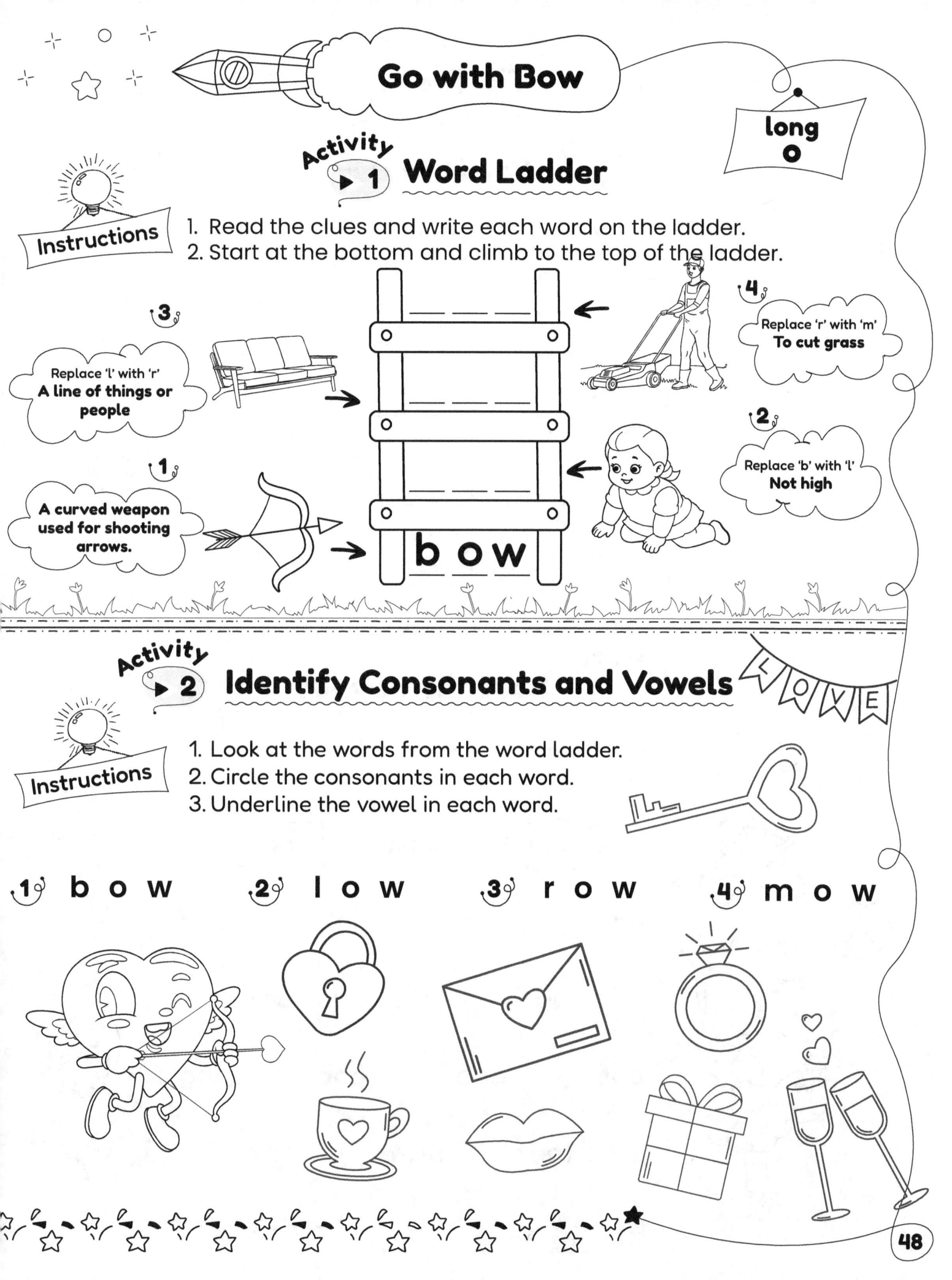

Tip Toe

Activity 1 — Word Ladder

1. Read the clues and write each word on the ladder.
2. Start at the bottom and climb to the top of the ladder.

3. Change 'f' to 'h'
A gardening tool

4. Change 'h' to 'd'
A female deer

2. Change 't' to 'f'
Another word for an enemy

1. **A part of your foot**

t o e

Activity 2 — Sort the Sounds

1. Draw an oval around the words with the short o sound.
2. Draw a rectangle around the words with the long o sound.

dog   box   hoe

hot   no   jot   bow

go   toe   dot

pot   doe   cob   log

foe   mow   fox

Activity 1 Word Ladder

Instructions

1. Read the clues and write each word on the ladder.
2. Start at the bottom and climb to the top of the ladder.

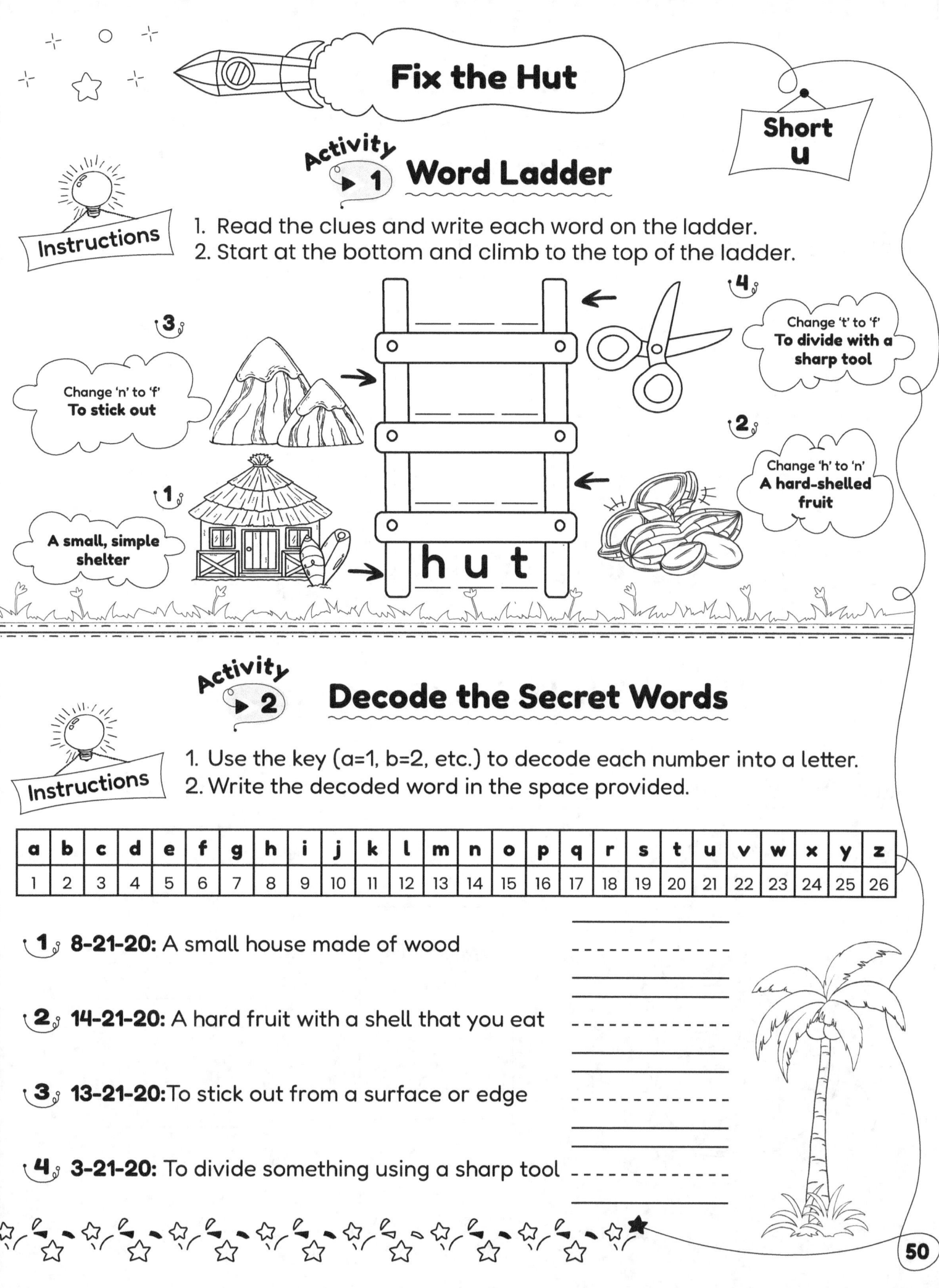

4 Change 't' to 'f'
To divide with a sharp tool

3 Change 'n' to 'f'
To stick out

2 Change 'h' to 'n'
A hard-shelled fruit

1 **A small, simple shelter**

h u t

Activity 2 Decode the Secret Words

Instructions

1. Use the key (a=1, b=2, etc.) to decode each number into a letter.
2. Write the decoded word in the space provided.

a	b	c	d	e	f	g	h	i	j	k	l	m	n	o	p	q	r	s	t	u	v	w	x	y	z
1	2	3	4	5	6	7	8	9	10	11	12	13	14	15	16	17	18	19	20	21	22	23	24	25	26

1. 8-21-20: A small house made of wood

_____

2. 14-21-20: A hard fruit with a shell that you eat

_____

3. 13-21-20: To stick out from a surface or edge

_____

4. 3-21-20: To divide something using a sharp tool

_____

Follow the Mud

Activity 1 — Word Ladder

Instructions

1. Read the clues and write each word on the ladder.
2. Start at the bottom and climb to the top of the ladder.

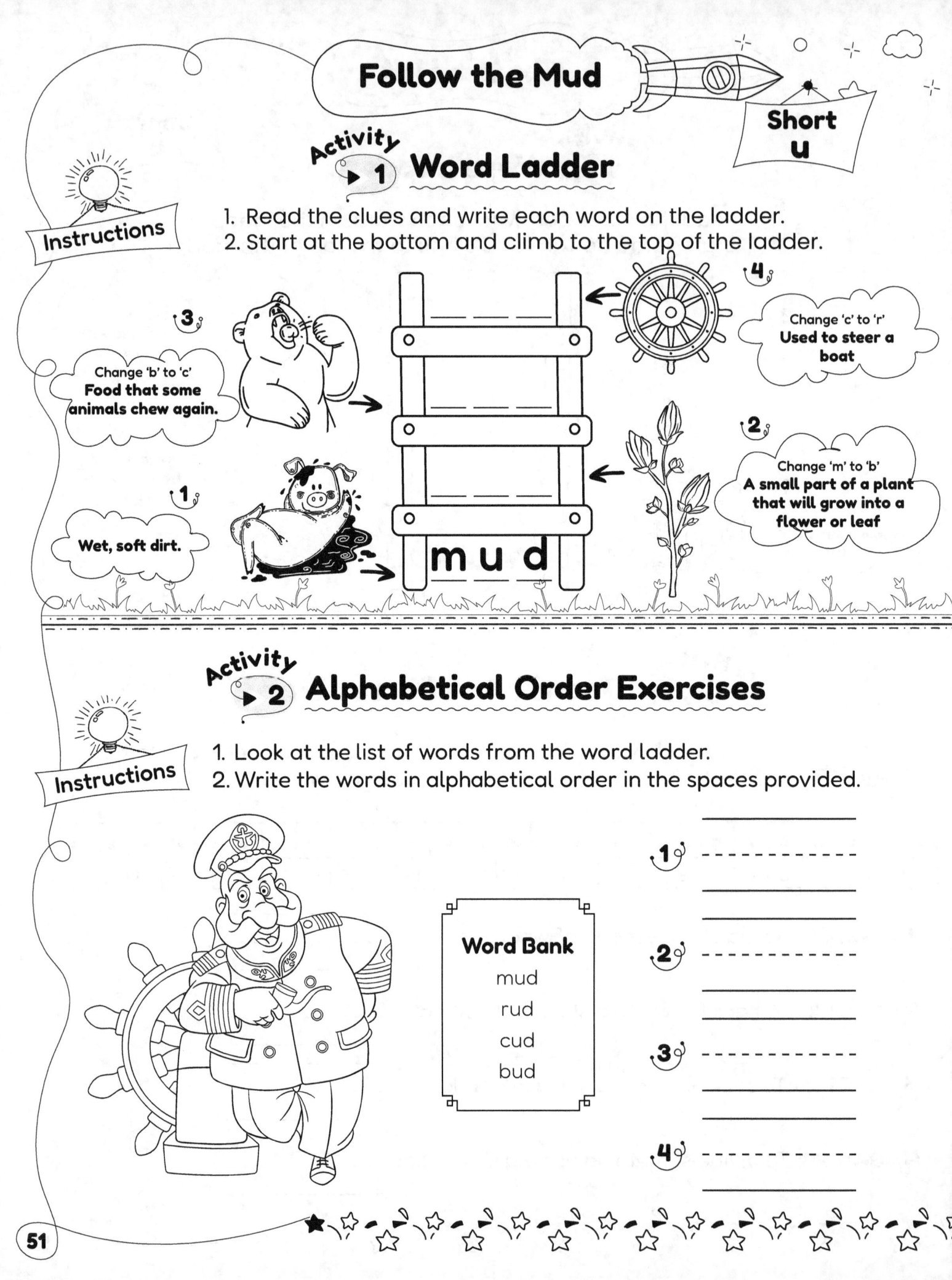

4. Change 'c' to 'r'
Used to steer a boat

3. Change 'b' to 'c'
Food that some animals chew again.

2. Change 'm' to 'b'
A small part of a plant that will grow into a flower or leaf

1. **Wet, soft dirt.**

m u d

Activity 2 — Alphabetical Order Exercises

Instructions

1. Look at the list of words from the word ladder.
2. Write the words in alphabetical order in the spaces provided.

Word Bank
mud
rud
cud
bud

1. - - - - - - - - - - -

2. - - - - - - - - - - -

3. - - - - - - - - - - -

4. - - - - - - - - - - -

Fun in the Sun

Activity ▶ 1 Word Ladder

Instructions
1. Read the clues and write each word on the ladder.
2. Start at the bottom and climb to the top of the ladder.

4 Change the first letter **A woman who lives a religious life.**

3 Change the first letter **Something that makes you happy.**

2 Change the first letter **to move quickly on your feet**

1 **A star that lights up the day.**

s u n

Activity ▶ 2 Word Matching

Instructions
1. Look at the pictures and the words.
2. Draw a line to match each word with the correct picture.

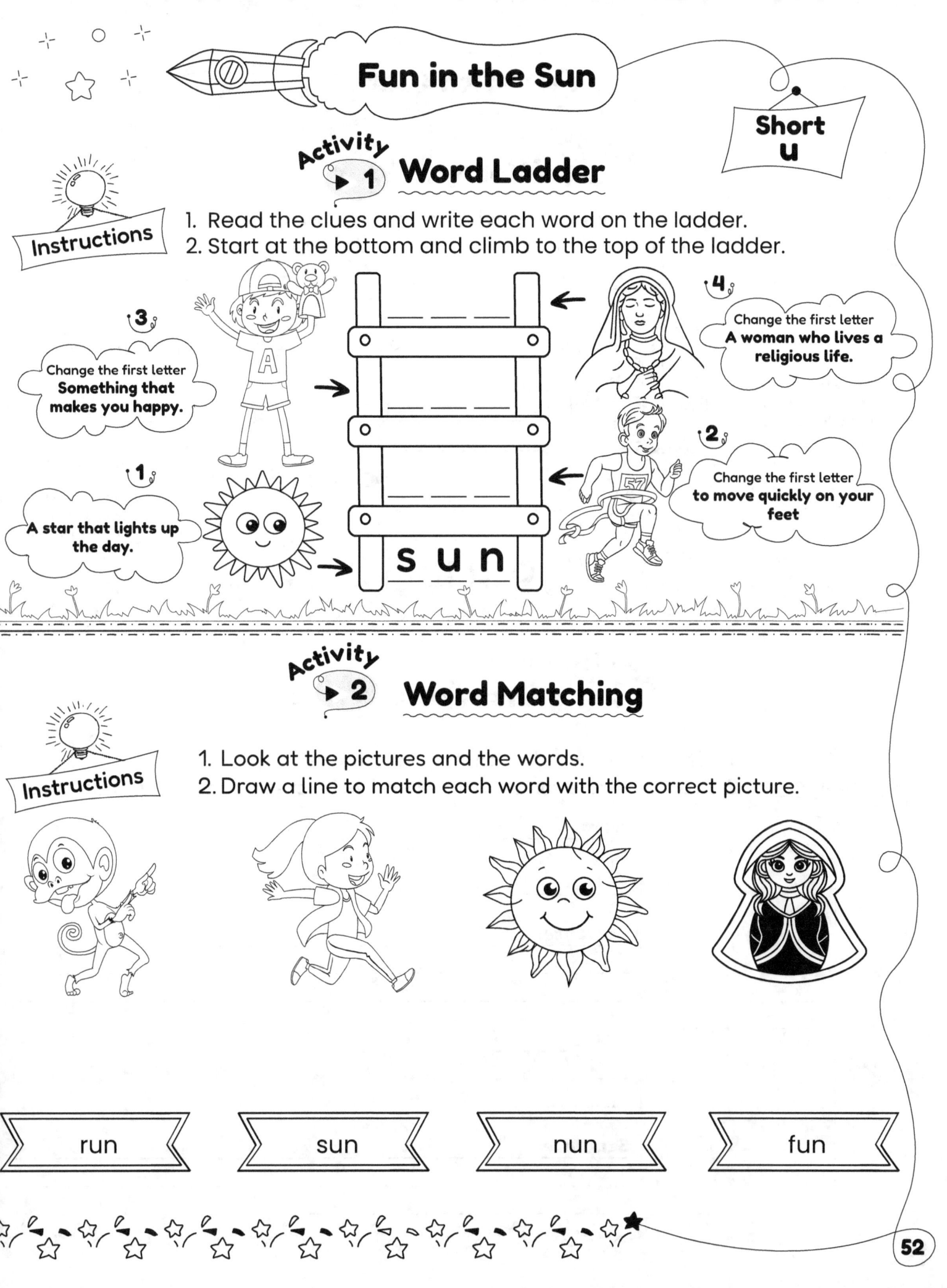

run   sun   nun   fun

52

Fun with Gum

Activity 1 Word Ladder

Instructions

1. Read the clues and write each word on the ladder.
2. Start at the bottom and climb to the top of the ladder.

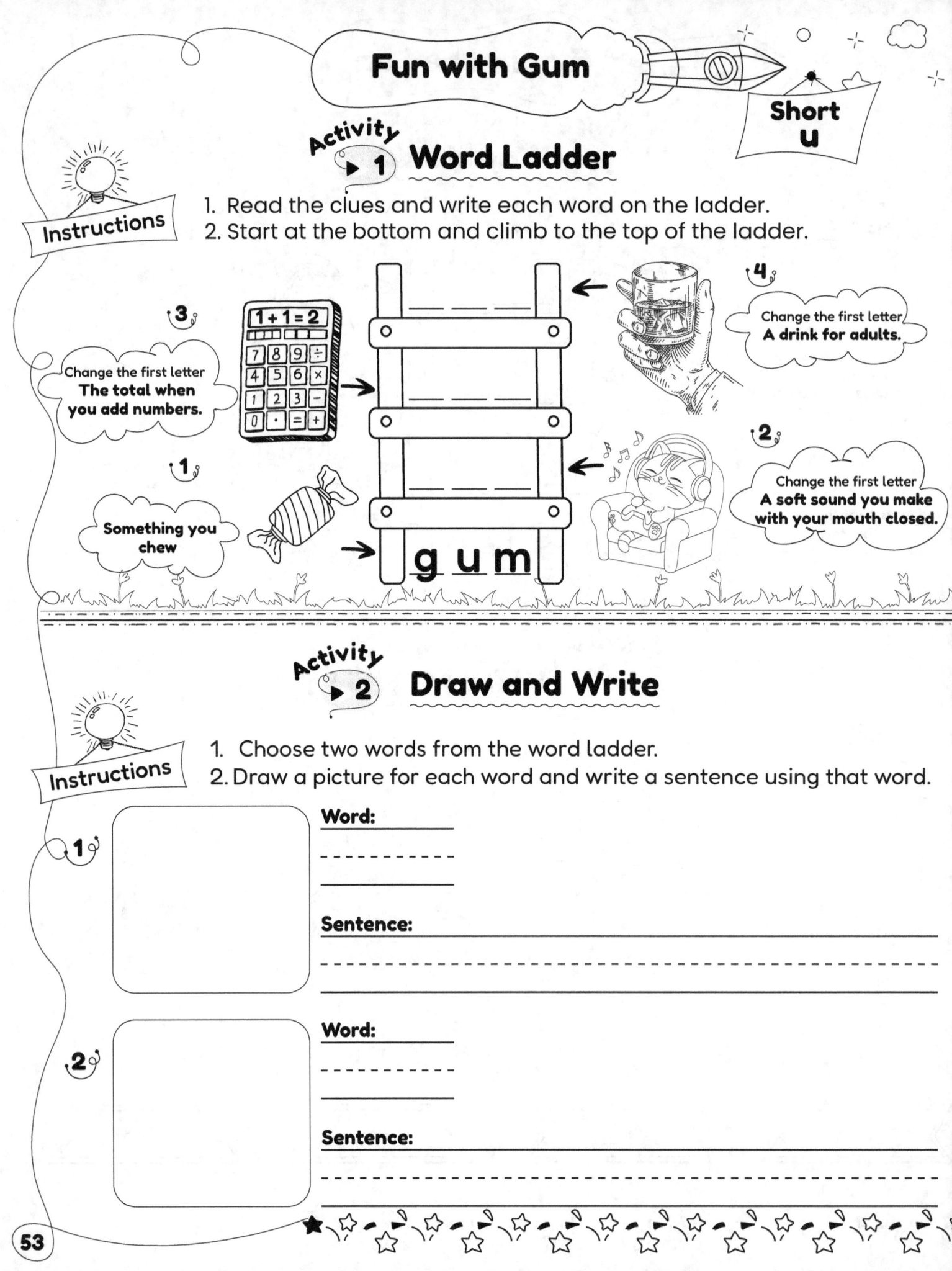

4 Change the first letter **A drink for adults.**

3 Change the first letter **The total when you add numbers.**

2 Change the first letter **A soft sound you make with your mouth closed.**

1 Something you chew

g u m

Activity 2 Draw and Write

Instructions

1. Choose two words from the word ladder.
2. Draw a picture for each word and write a sentence using that word.

1

Word: _ _ _ _ _ _ _ _ _

Sentence: _____

2

Word: _ _ _ _ _ _ _ _ _

Sentence: _____

53

Play with Jug

Activity ▶ 1 Word Ladder

Instructions

1. Read the clues and write each word on the ladder.
2. Start at the bottom and climb to the top of the ladder.

4 Change 'p' to 'h'
What you do to show someone you care

3 Change 'm' to 'p'
A small breed of dog

2 Change 'j' to 'm'
A cup with a handle used for drinking

1 A container for holding liquids

j u g

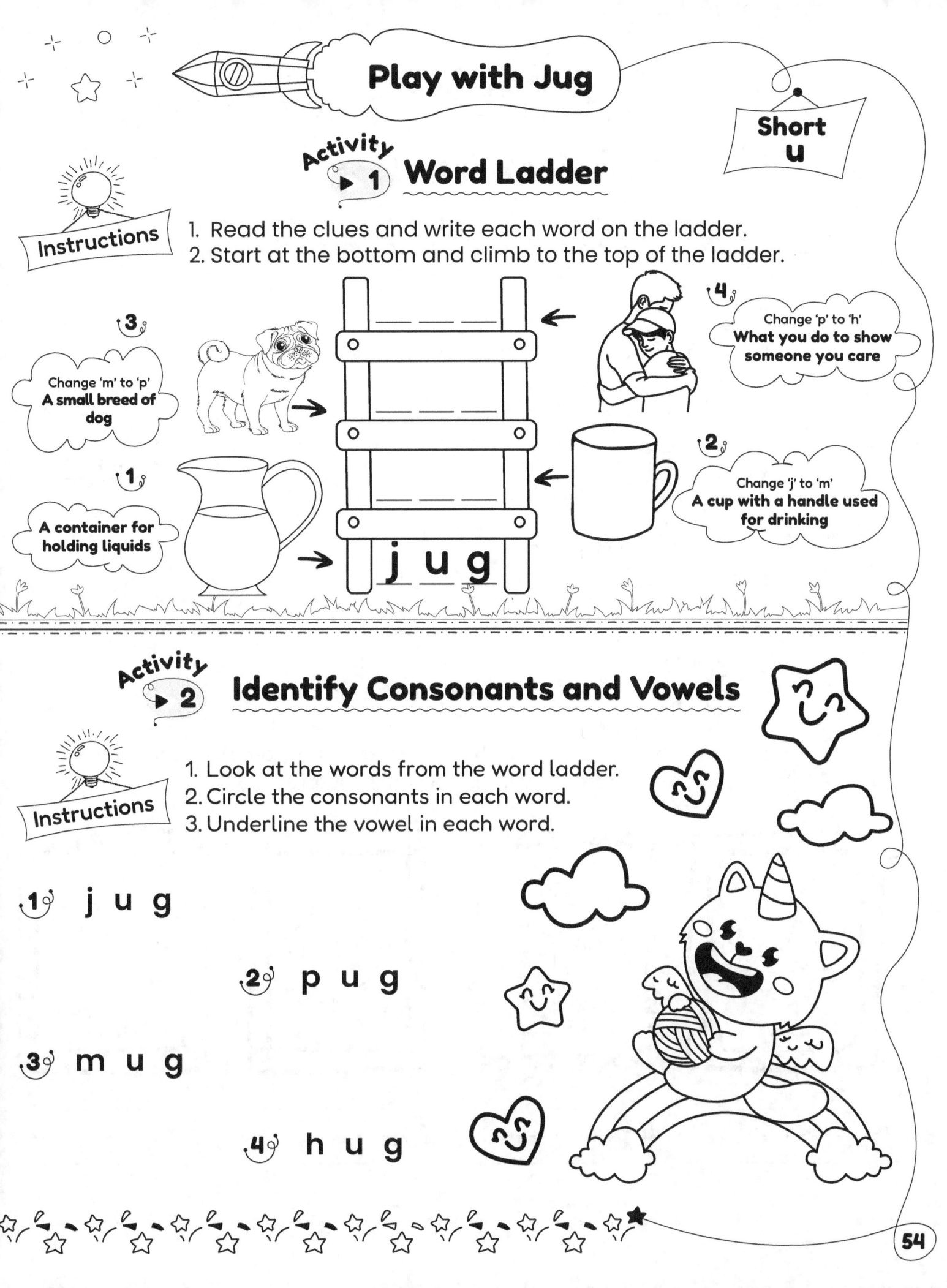

Activity ▶ 2 Identify Consonants and Vowels

Instructions

1. Look at the words from the word ladder.
2. Circle the consonants in each word.
3. Underline the vowel in each word.

1 j u g

2 p u g

3 m u g

4 h u g

Riding the Bus

Activity 1 — Word Ladder

1. Read the clues and write each word on the ladder.
2. Start at the bottom and climb to the top of the ladder.

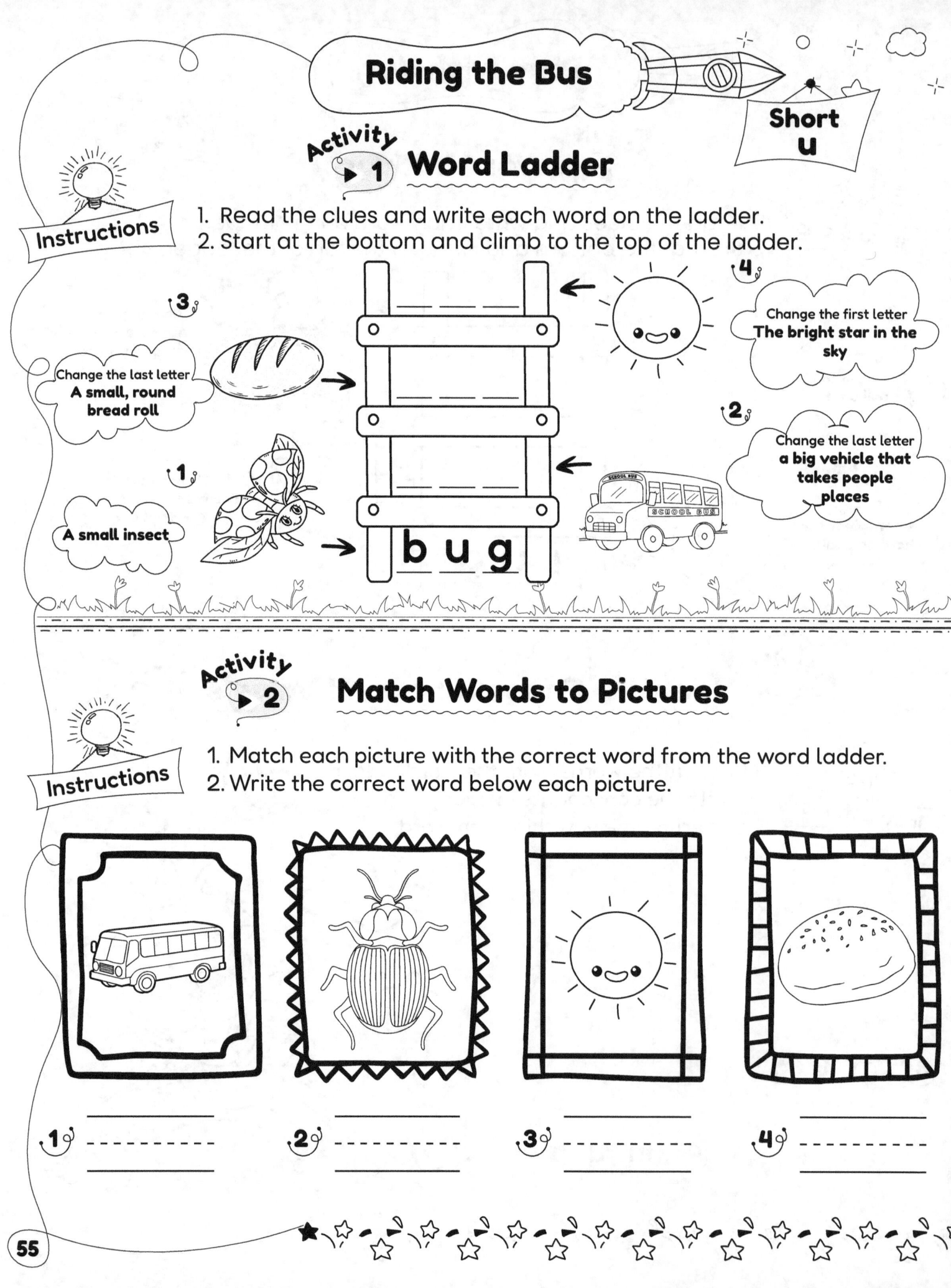

3 Change the last letter
A small, round bread roll

4 Change the first letter
The bright star in the sky

2 Change the last letter
a big vehicle that takes people places

1 A small insect

b u g

Activity 2 — Match Words to Pictures

1. Match each picture with the correct word from the word ladder.
2. Write the correct word below each picture.

1 _____

2 _____

3 _____

4 _____

What's in the Cup

Activity 1 Word Ladder

Instructions
1. Read the clues and write each word on the ladder.
2. Start at the bottom and climb to the top of the ladder.

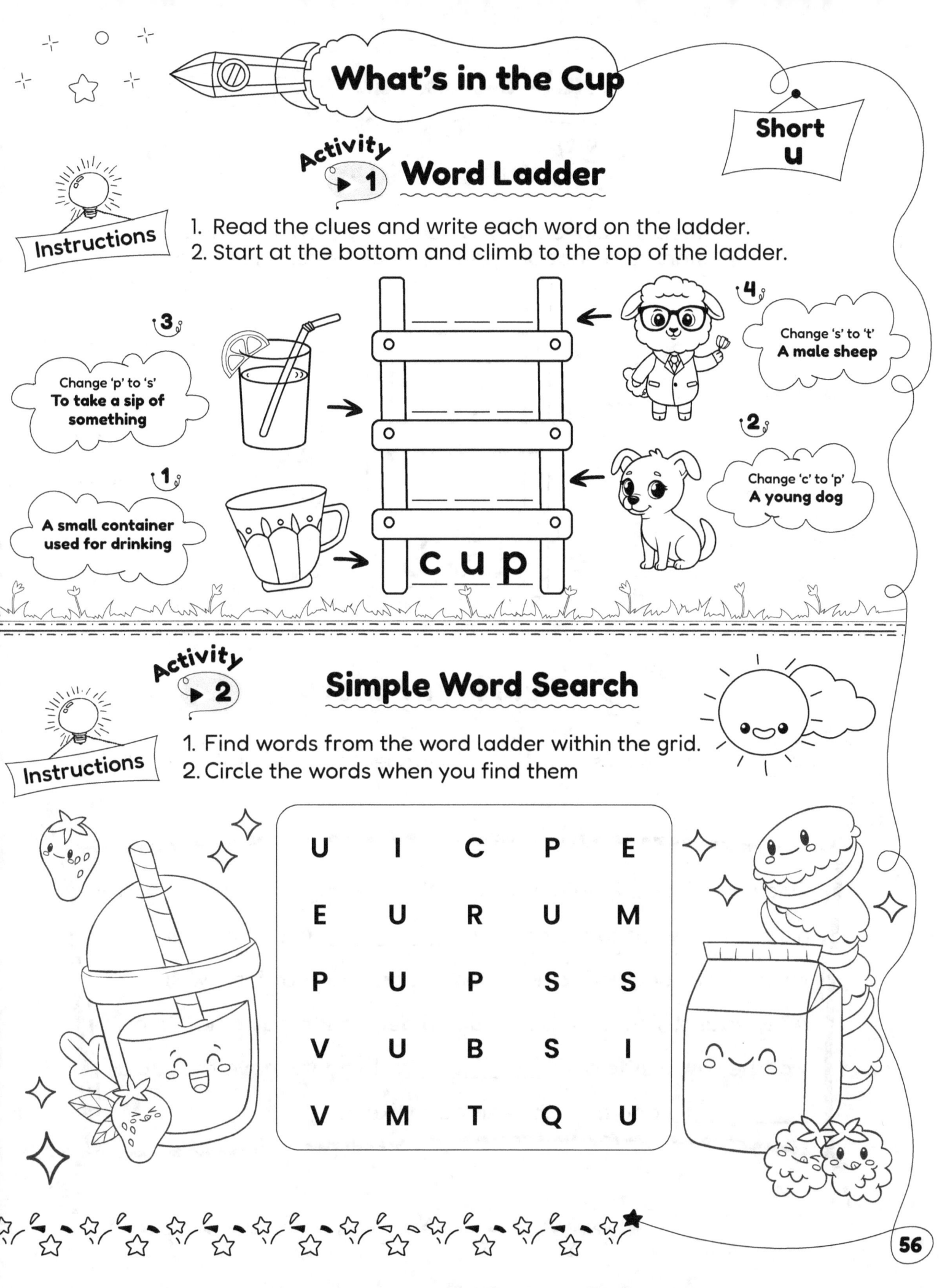

4 Change 's' to 't'
A male sheep

3 Change 'p' to 's'
To take a sip of something

2 Change 'c' to 'p'
A young dog

1 A small container used for drinking

c u p

Activity 2 Simple Word Search

Instructions
1. Find words from the word ladder within the grid.
2. Circle the words when you find them

U	I	C	P	E
E	U	R	U	M
P	U	P	S	S
V	U	B	S	I
V	M	T	Q	U

56

Rub-a-Dub Cub!

Activity 1 Word Ladder

1. Read the clues and write each word on the ladder.
2. Start at the bottom and climb to the top of the ladder.

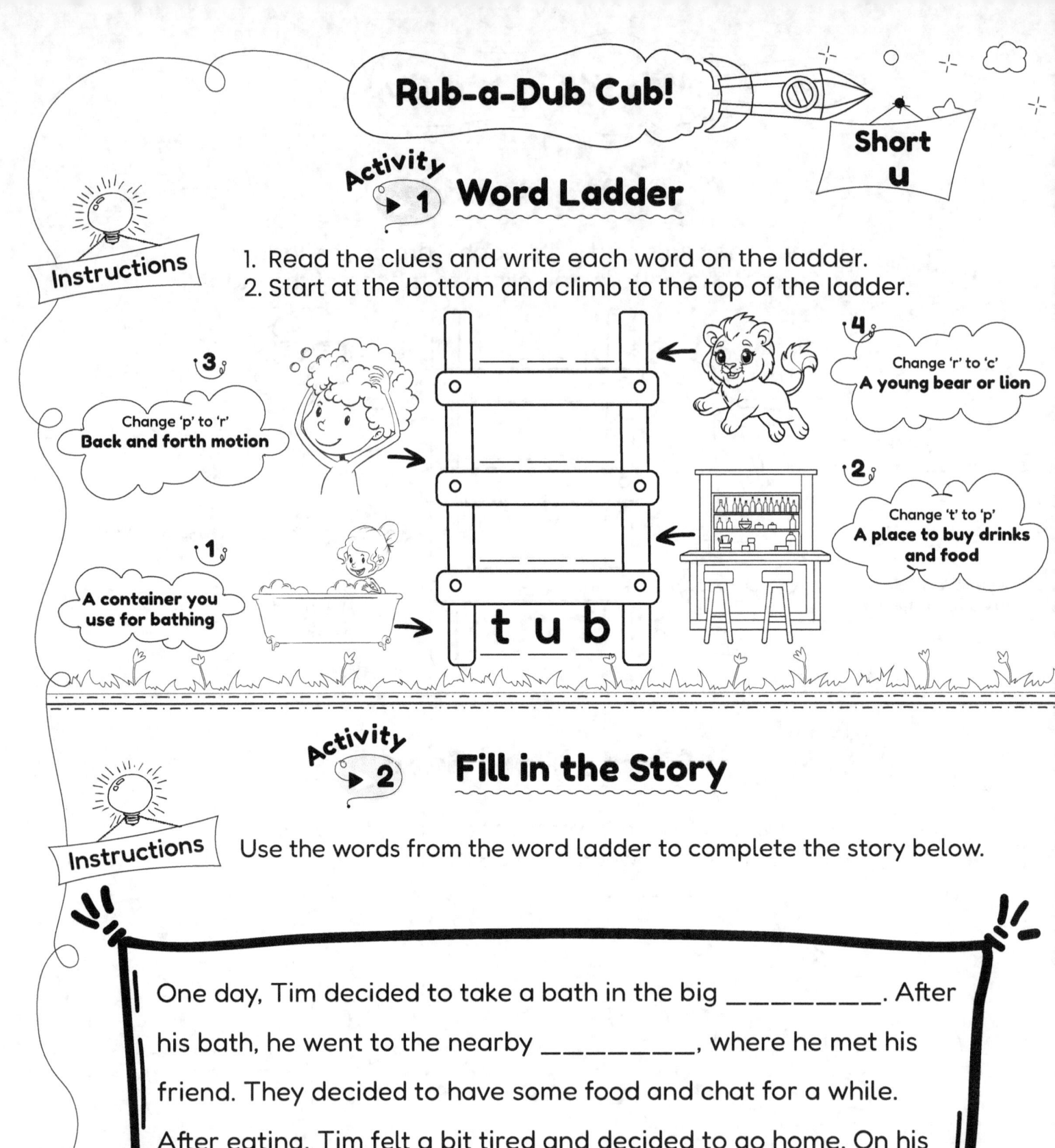

4 Change 'r' to 'c'
A young bear or lion

3 Change 'p' to 'r'
Back and forth motion

2 Change 't' to 'p'
A place to buy drinks and food

1 A container you use for bathing

t u b

Activity 2 Fill in the Story

Use the words from the word ladder to complete the story below.

One day, Tim decided to take a bath in the big _____. After his bath, he went to the nearby _____, where he met his friend. They decided to have some food and chat for a while. After eating, Tim felt a bit tired and decided to go home. On his way, he saw a little bear _____. He gently gave the cub a _____, and the cub seemed to like it.

Lucky Duck

Activity 1 — Word Ladder

Instructions

1. Read the clues and write each word on the ladder.
2. Start at the bottom and climb to the top of the ladder.

4 Change 'b' to 't'
To fold or push into a small space.

3 Change 'l' to 'b'
A male deer

2 Change 'd' to 'l'
Good fortune

1 A bird that swims and quacks.

d u c k

Activity 2 — Color the Words

Instructions

Find the word that matches the picture and color it.

duck   dock   luck   lock   back   buck   tack   tuck

Rug Race

Activity ▸ 1 Word Ladder

1. Read the clues and write each word on the ladder.
2. Start at the bottom and climb to the top of the ladder.

4 Change 'l' to 'd'
Past tense of digging

3 Change 't' to 'l'
To drag something heavy

2 Change 'r' to 't'
To pull something hard

1 A small carpet

r u g

Activity ▸ 2 Rhyming Words Activity

Draw a picture of your favorite word that rhymes with 'rug'.

rug

Bake a Cake

Activity ▶ 1 Word Ladder

Instructions
1. Read the clues and write each word on the ladder.
2. Start at the bottom and climb to the top of the ladder.

3 Change 'g' to 'n'
A stick used while walking

1 **A sweet baked dessert**

4 Change 'n' to 's'
A container for holding something

2 Change 'k' to 'g'
A structure for keeping animals

c a k e

Activity ▶ 2 Trace and Write the Words

Instructions
1. Trace each word from the word ladder in the space provided.
2. Practice writing each word on your own.

1 <u>cake</u>

2 <u>cane</u>

3 <u>case</u>

4 <u>cage</u>

Say It Loud

Activity ▶ 1 Word Ladder

long a (ay)

Instructions

1. Read the clues and write each word on the ladder.
2. Start at the bottom and climb to the top of the ladder.

3 Change 'b' to 'h'
Dried grass

1 To speak words

4 Change 'h' to 'p'
To give money for something

2 Change 's' to 'b'
A body of water surrounded by land

s a y

Activity ▶ 2 Sort Words into Categories

Instructions

Write each word in the correct category.

Actions	Word Bank	Things
	pay	
	bay	
	hay	
	say	

Seal the Deal

Activity 1 Word Ladder

Instructions

1. Read the clues and write each word on the ladder.
2. Start at the bottom and climb to the top of the ladder.

3 Change 'd' to 'm'
Food eaten at a particular time

4 Change 'm' to 's'
A marine animal

1 Genuine or true

2 Change 'r' to 'd'
An agreement

r e a l

Activity 2 Draw and Write

Instructions

1. Choose two words from the word ladder.
2. Draw a picture for each word and write a sentence using that word.

1

Word: _ _ _ _ _ _ _ _ _ _

Sentence: _____

2

Word: _ _ _ _ _ _ _ _ _ _

Sentence: _____

62

Pie in the Sky

long i
(ie)

Activity 1 Word Ladder

Instructions

1. Read the clues and write each word on the ladder.
2. Start at the bottom and climb to the top of the ladder.

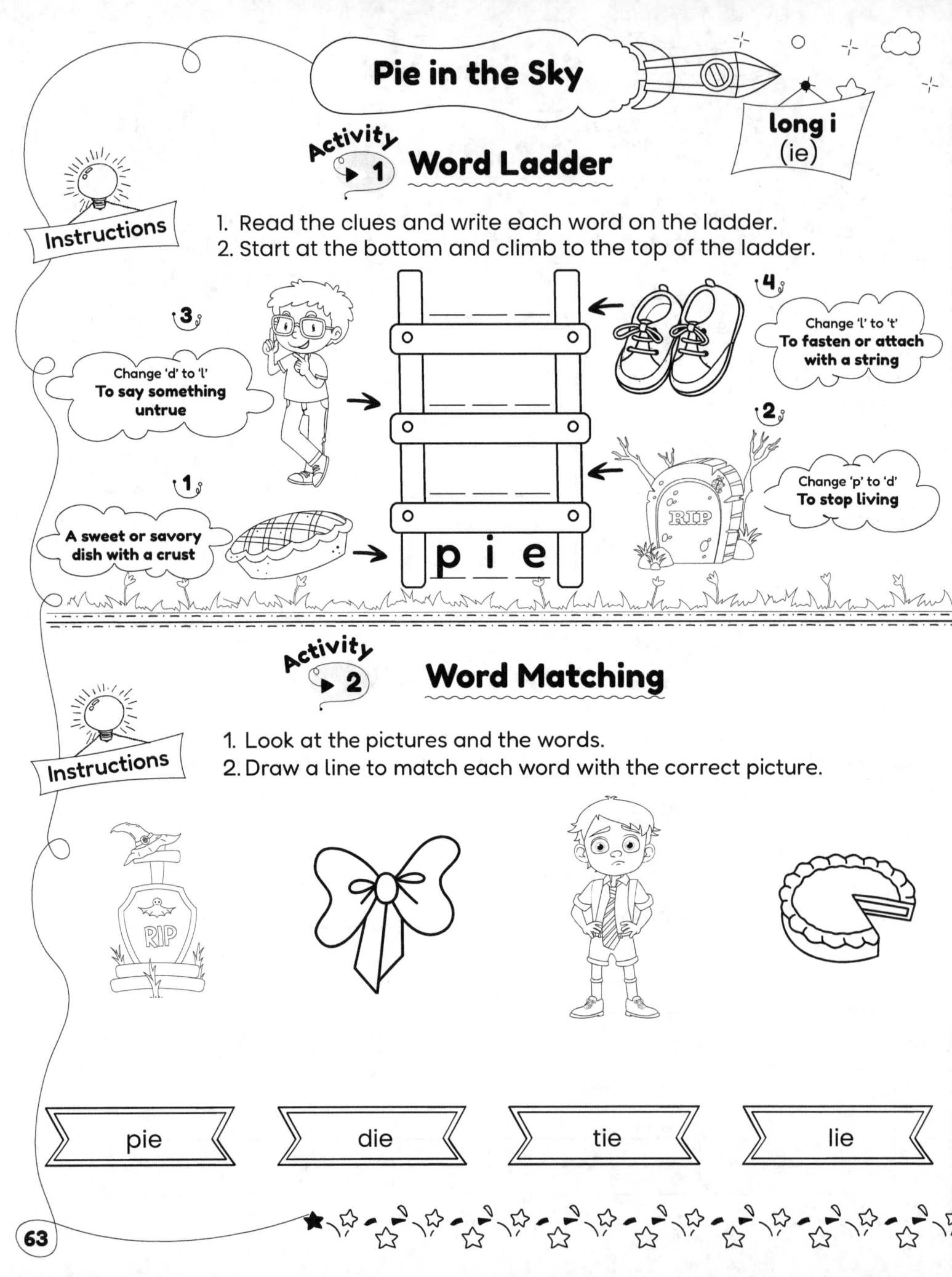

4
Change 'l' to 't'
To fasten or attach with a string

3
Change 'd' to 'l'
To say something untrue

2
Change 'p' to 'd'
To stop living

1
A sweet or savory dish with a crust

p i e

Activity 2 Word Matching

Instructions

1. Look at the pictures and the words.
2. Draw a line to match each word with the correct picture.

pie   die   tie   lie

Food for Thought

Activity ▶ 1 Word Ladder

Instructions

1. Read the clues and write each word on the ladder.
2. Start at the bottom and climb to the top of the ladder.

3 Change 'd' to 'n'
The natural satellite of Earth

4 Change 'm' to 's'
In a short time

2 Change 'f' to 'm'
A state of feeling

1 Something you eat

f o o d

Activity ▶ 2 Alphabetical Order Exercises

Instructions

1. Look at the list of words from the word ladder.
2. Write the words in alphabetical order in the spaces provided.

1 _____

2 _____

3 _____

4 _____

Word Bank
mood
food
soon
moon

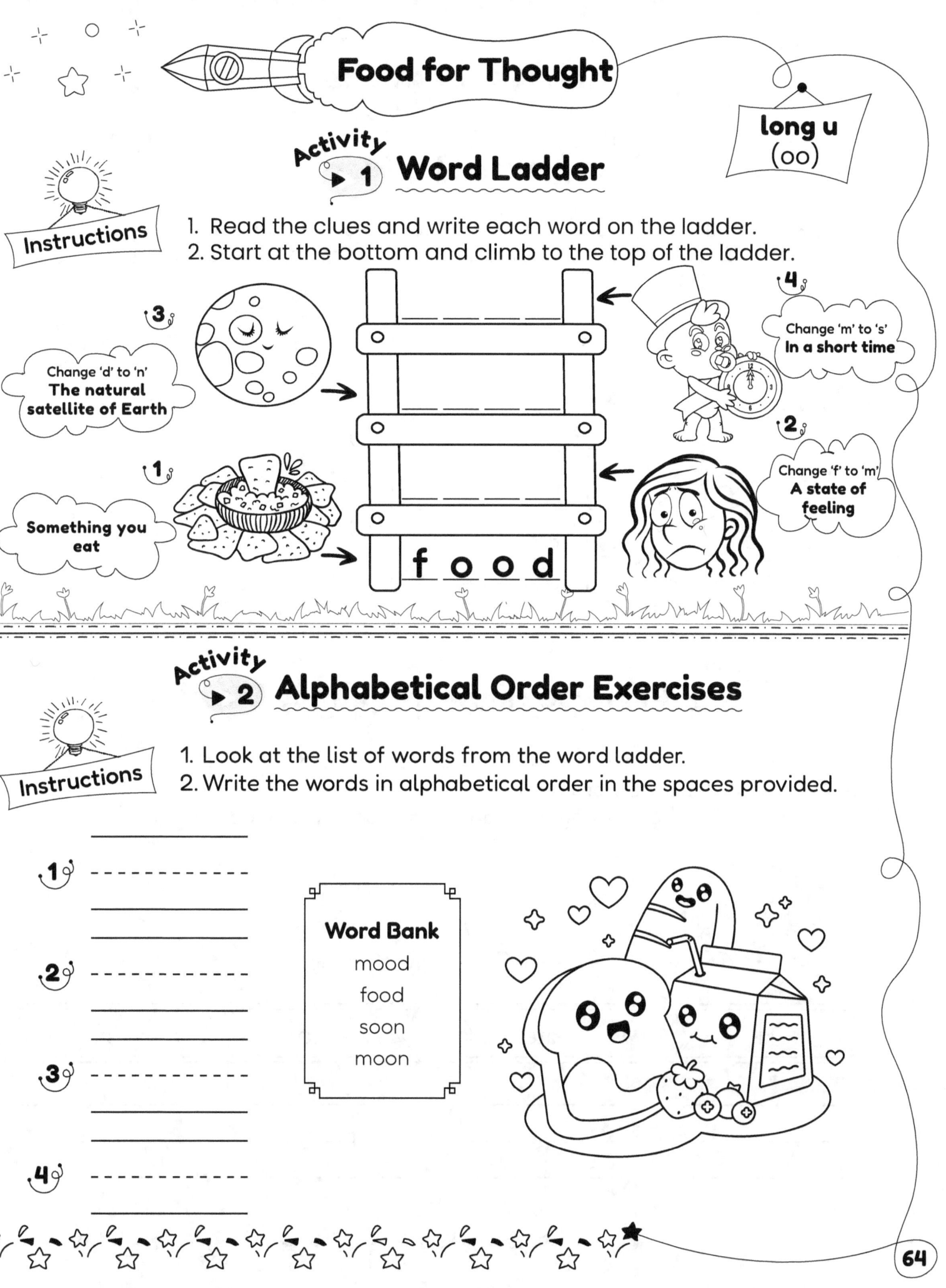

64

Kite Kit Creations

Activity 1 — Word Ladder

1. Read the clues and write each word on the ladder.
2. Start at the bottom and climb to the top of the ladder.

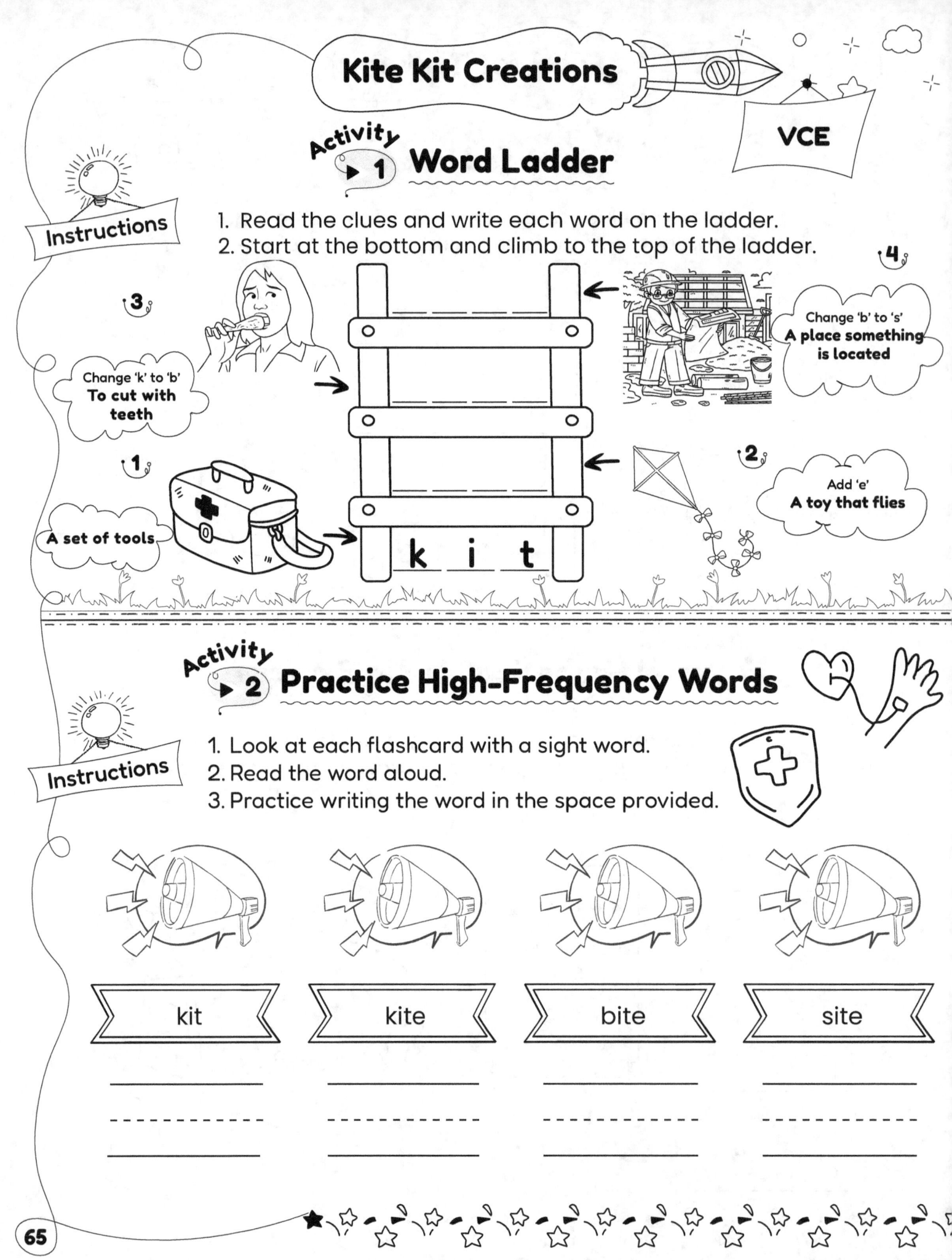

3. Change 'k' to 'b'
To cut with teeth

4. Change 'b' to 's'
A place something is located

1. **A set of tools**

2. Add 'e'
A toy that flies

k   i   t

Activity 2 — Practice High-Frequency Words

1. Look at each flashcard with a sight word.
2. Read the word aloud.
3. Practice writing the word in the space provided.

kit

kite

bite

site

Hopeful Hops

Activity 1 Word Ladder

VCE

Instructions

1. Read the clues and write each word on the ladder.
2. Start at the bottom and climb to the top of the ladder.

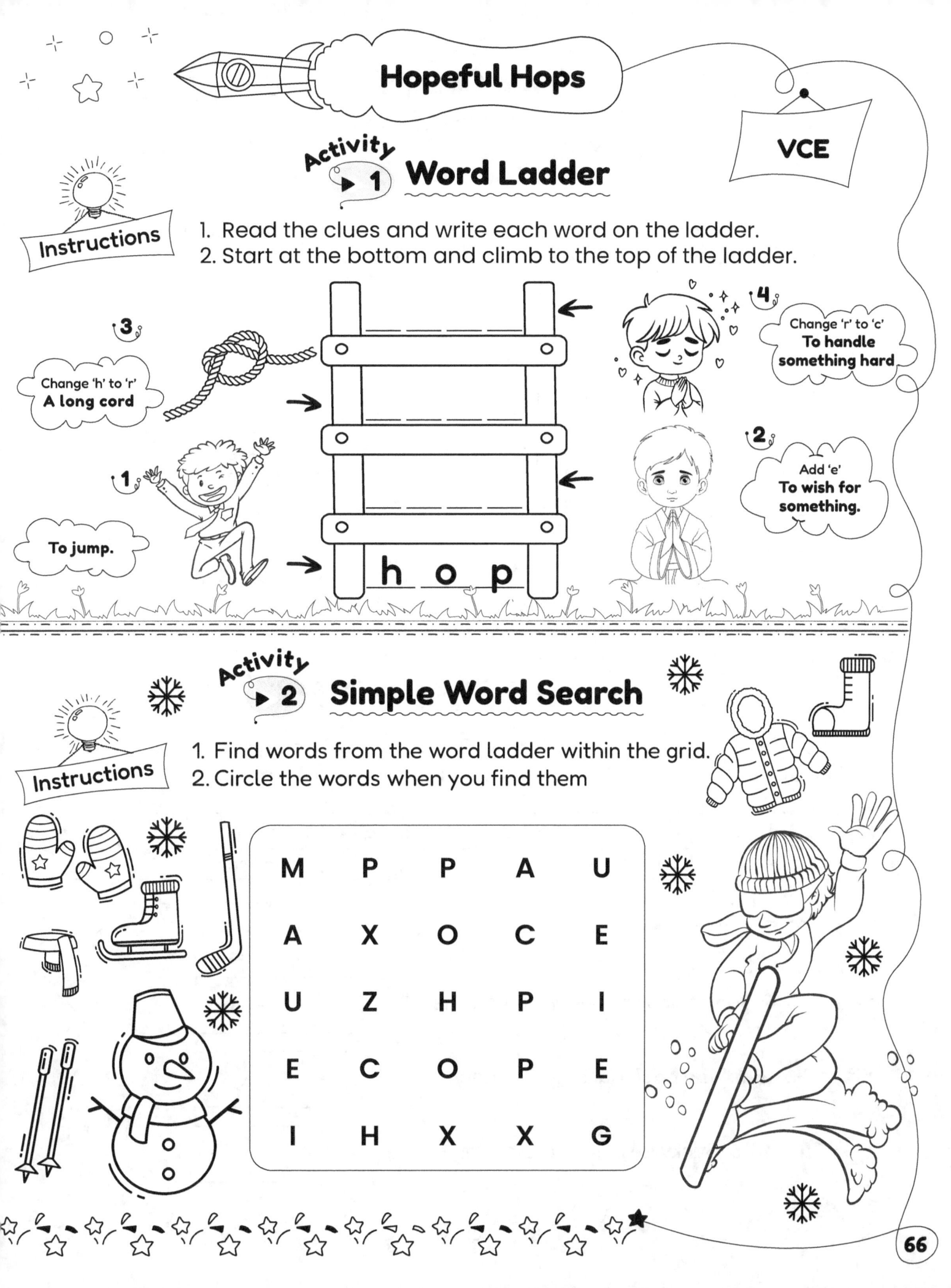

3 Change 'h' to 'r'
A long cord

1 To jump.

4 Change 'r' to 'c'
To handle something hard

2 Add 'e'
To wish for something.

h o p

Activity 2 Simple Word Search

Instructions

1. Find words from the word ladder within the grid.
2. Circle the words when you find them

M	P	P	A	U
A	X	O	C	E
U	Z	H	P	I
E	C	O	P	E
I	H	X	X	G

Cape Capers

Activity 1 — Word Ladder

1. Read the clues and write each word on the ladder.
2. Start at the bottom and climb to the top of the ladder.

3. Change 'c' to 't' — A sticky strip

4. Change 't' to 'n' — The back of the neck

1. You wear on your head

2. Add 'e' — Worn over the shoulders

c a p

Activity 2 — Decode the Secret Words

1. Use the key (a=1, b=2, etc.) to decode each number into a letter.
2. Write the decoded word in the space provided.

a	b	c	d	e	f	g	h	i	j	k	l	m	n	o	p	q	r	s	t	u	v	w	x	y	z
1	2	3	4	5	6	7	8	9	10	11	12	13	14	15	16	17	18	19	20	21	22	23	24	25	26

1. **3-1-16-5:** A clothing you wear on your shoulders. - - - - - - - - - - - - -

2. **3-1-16:** Something you wear on your head. - - - - - - - - - - - -

3. **14-1-16-5:** The back part of your neck. - - - - - - - - - - - -

4. **20-1-16-5:** Sticky strip for holding things - - - - - - - - - - - -

Pine Time

Activity 1 — Word Ladder

1. Read the clues and write each word on the ladder.
2. Start at the bottom and climb to the top of the ladder.

3 Change 'd' to 'n'
Belongs to me

1 A small, sharp fastener

4 Change 'm' to 's'
The number after eight

2 Change 'f' to 'm'
A type of tree

p i n

Activity 2 — Fill in the Blanks

1. Complete each sentence with a word from the word bank.
2. Write the word in the blank space.

1 The _____ tree is very tall.

2 He is _____ years old.

3 She used a _____ to fasten the paper.

4 That toy is _____ , not yours.

Word Bank

mine
pine
nine
pin

Code Mode Magic

Activity 1 Word Ladder

Instructions

1. Read the clues and write each word on the ladder.
2. Start at the top and climb to the top of the ladder.

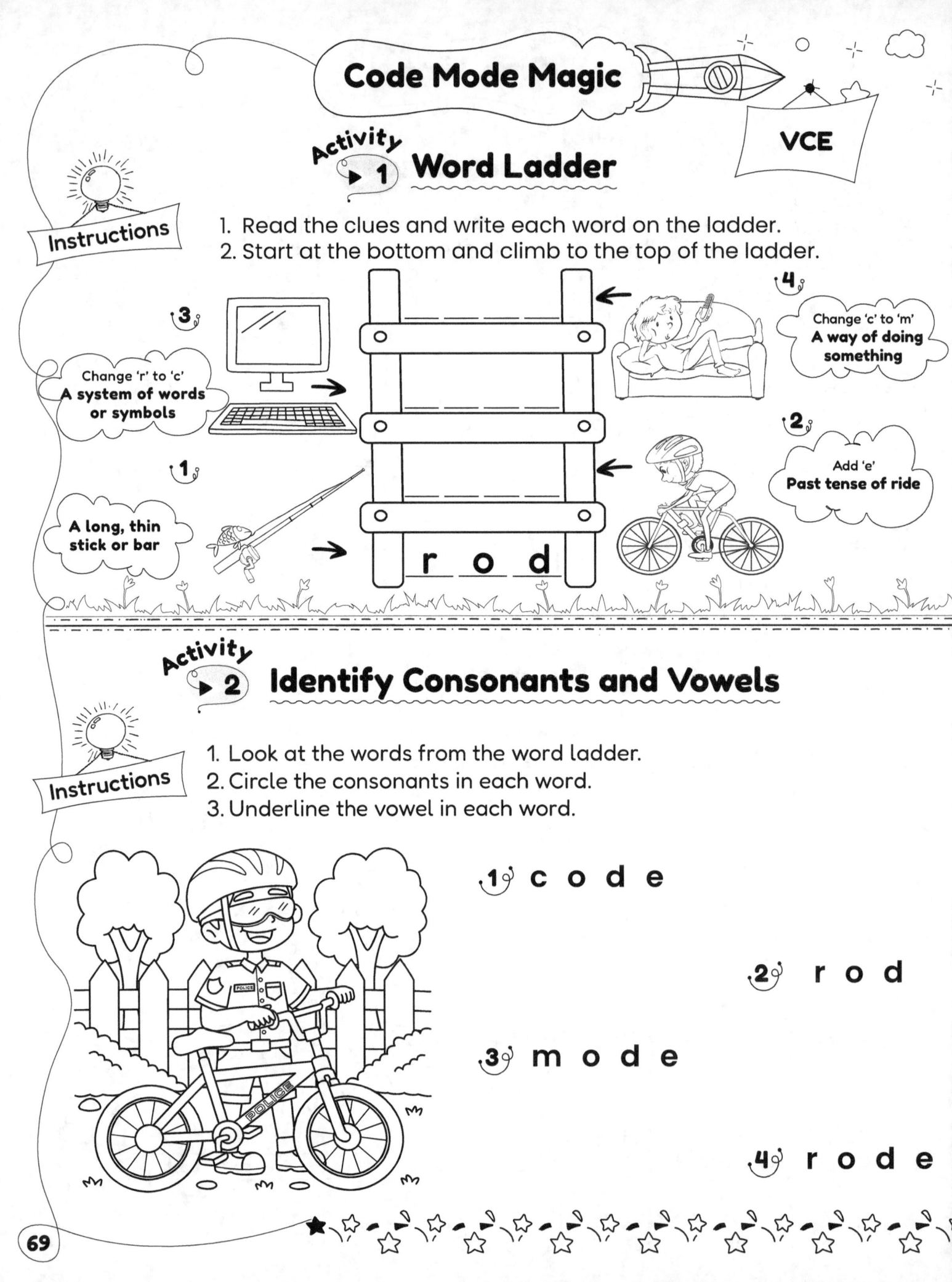

3 Change 'r' to 'c'
A system of words or symbols

1 A long, thin stick or bar

4 Change 'c' to 'm'
A way of doing something

2 Add 'e'
Past tense of ride

r o d

Activity 2 Identify Consonants and Vowels

Instructions

1. Look at the words from the word ladder.
2. Circle the consonants in each word.
3. Underline the vowel in each word.

1 c o d e

2 r o d

3 m o d e

4 r o d e

Trek to Cure

Activity ▶1 Word Ladder

Instructions

1. Read the clues and write each word on the ladder.
2. Start at the bottom and climb to the top of the ladder.

4 Change 'b' to 'r' **Makes an illness go away**

3 Change 't' to 'c' **A solid shape with six square faces**

2 Add 'e' **A long, hollow cylinder**

1 You bathe in it

t u b

Activity ▶2 Trace and Write the Words

Instructions

1. Trace each word from the word ladder in the space provided.
2. Practice writing each word on your own.

1 tub

2 cure

3 tube

4 cube

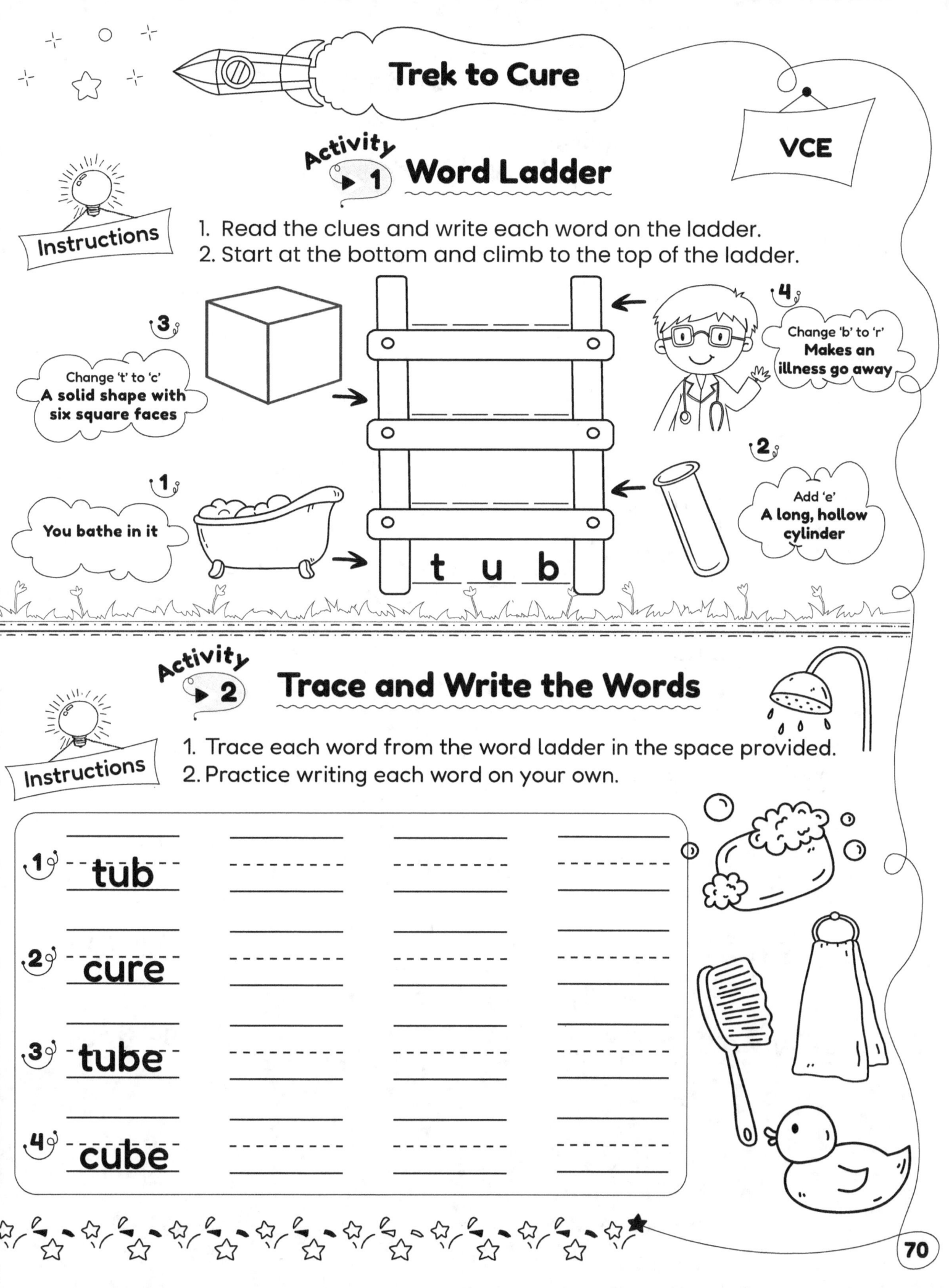

70

Winning Wonders

Activity 1 — Word Ladder

1. Read the clues and write each word on the ladder.
2. Start at the bottom and climb to the top of the ladder.

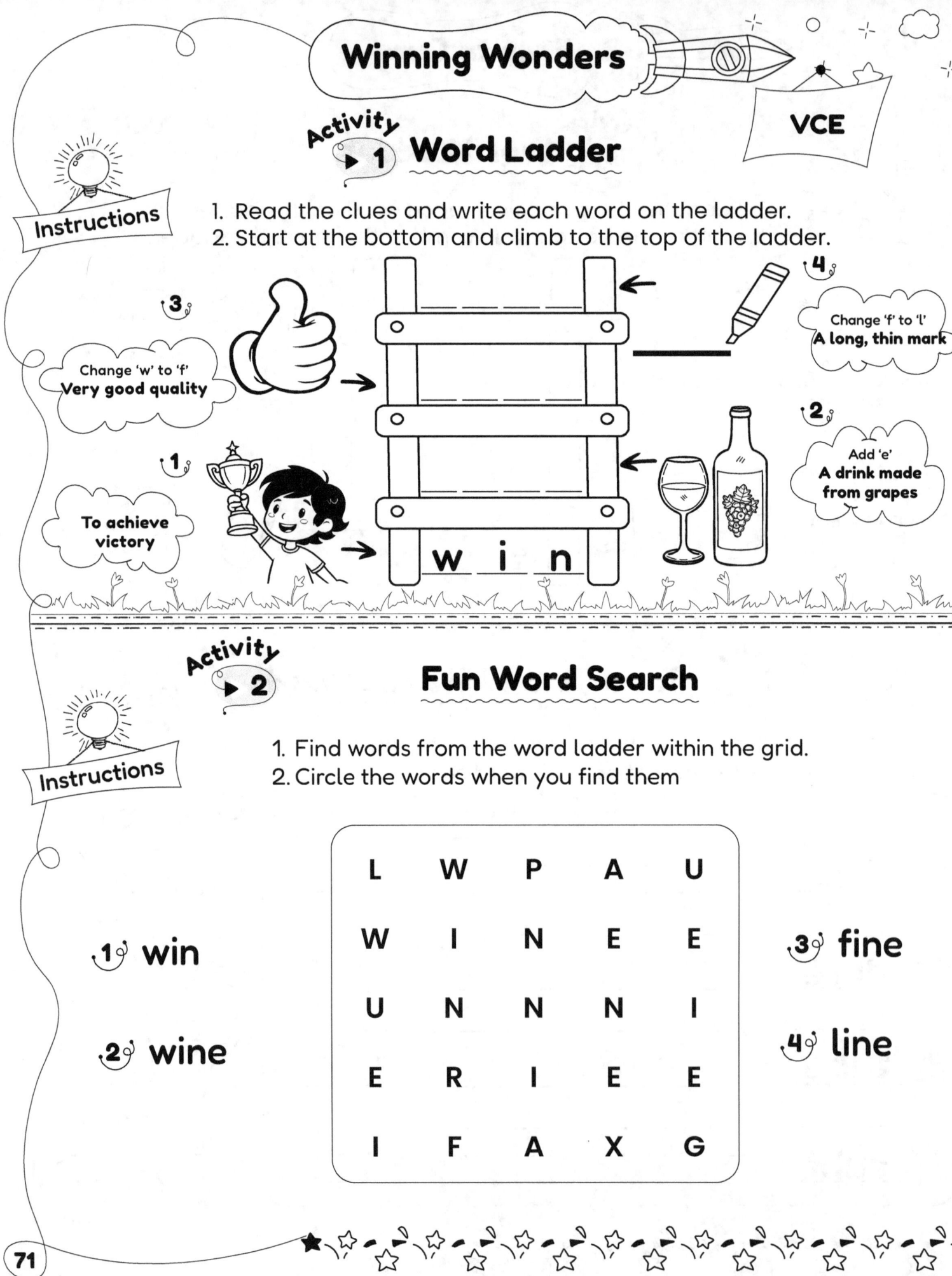

3 Change 'w' to 'f'
Very good quality

4 Change 'f' to 'l'
A long, thin mark

1 To achieve victory

2 Add 'e'
A drink made from grapes

w i n

Activity 2 — Fun Word Search

1. Find words from the word ladder within the grid.
2. Circle the words when you find them

1 win

2 wine

3 fine

4 line

L	W	P	A	U
W	I	N	E	E
U	N	N	N	I
E	R	I	E	E
I	F	A	X	G

Race with the Rat

Activity ▶ 1 Word Ladder

1. Read the clues and write each word on the ladder.
2. Start at the bottom and climb to the top of the ladder.

3 Change 'r' to 'l'
Not on time

4 Change 'l' to 'g'
A door in a fence

1
A small rodent

2 Add 'e'
How fast something is

r a t

Activity ▶ 2 Fill in the Story

Use the words from the word ladder to complete the story below.

One day, a little _____ ran through the _____. He was trying to find his way home before it got _____. He needed to check the _____ to see if he was on time.

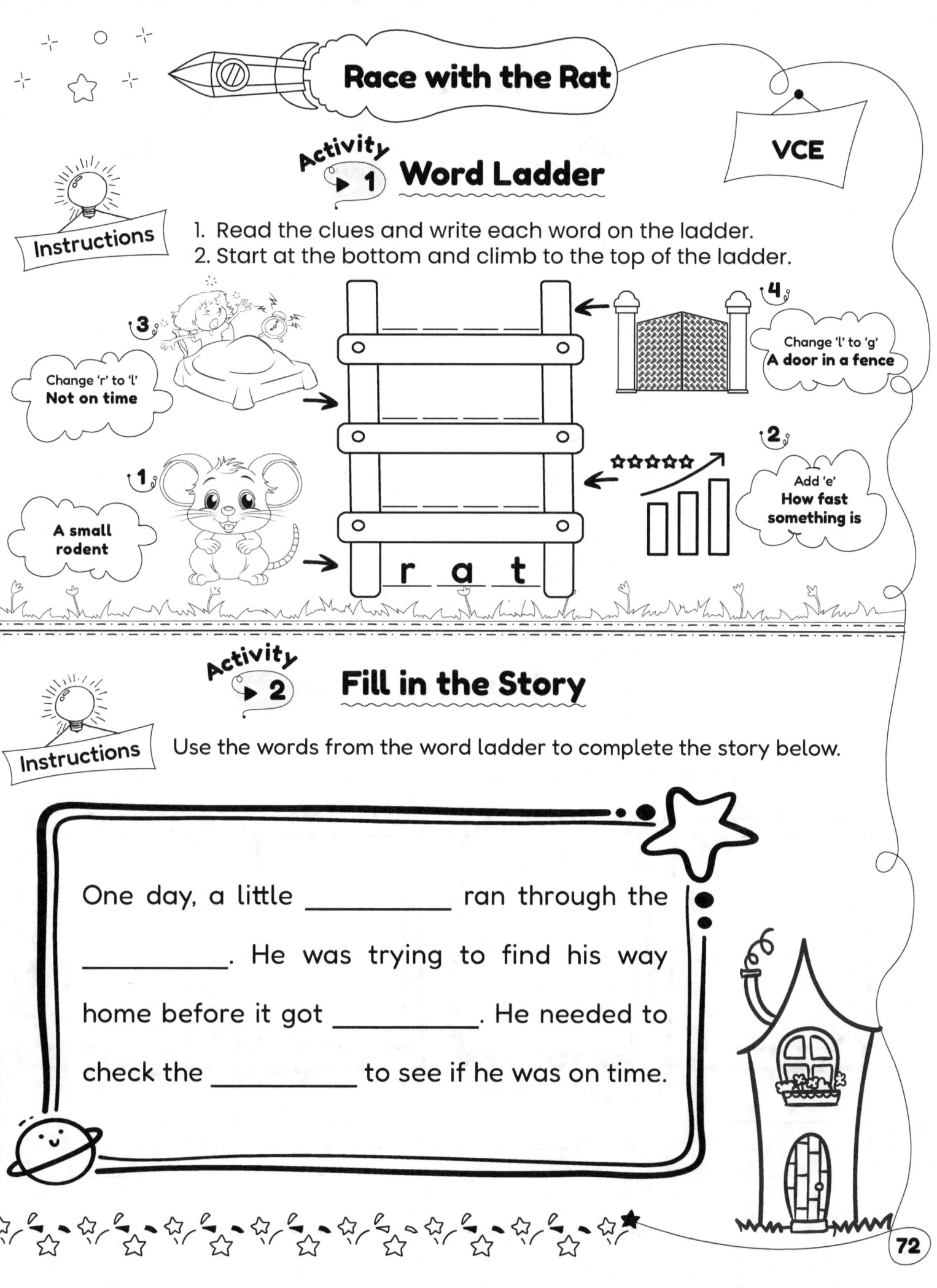

Hats Off

Activity 1 — Word Ladder

1. Read the clues and write each word on the ladder.
2. Start at the bottom and climb to the top of the ladder.

3 Change 'h' to 'm'
A friend or partner

4 Change 'm' to 'd'
A specific day of the month

1 **You wear on your head**

2 Add 'e'
To feel strong dislike

h a t

Activity 2 — Draw the Words

1. Draw a picture of each word from the word bank.
2. Label your drawings with the correct word.

1. _ _ _ _ _ _ _ _ _

2. _ _ _ _ _ _ _ _ _

3. _ _ _ _ _ _ _ _ _

4. _ _ _ _ _ _ _ _ _

Sunny Adventures

Activity 1 — Word Ladder

Instructions

1. Read the clues and write each word on the ladder.
2. Start at the bottom and climb to the top of the ladder.

VCE

3 Change 's' to 'n'. Add 'e'
Not any

1 The star in the sky

4 Change 'n' to 'd'
Finished

2 Change 'u' to 'o'
A boy in a family

s u n

Activity 2 — Draw and Write

Instructions

1. Choose two words from the word ladder.
2. Draw a picture for each word and write a sentence using that word.

1

Word: _____

Sentence: _____

2

Word: _____

Sentence: _____

74

Band and Beyond

Activity 1 — Word Ladder

Instructions

1. Read the clues and write each word on the ladder.
2. Start at the bottom and climb to the top of the ladder.

3 Change the first letter
Tiny grains on a beach

4 Change the first letter
Solid ground

1 Group of musicians

2 Change the first letter
End of your arm

b a n d

Activity 2 — Find the Blends

Instructions

Color the drum with words that have consonant blends.

band

hen

hand

sand

cat

land

pug

wand

dog

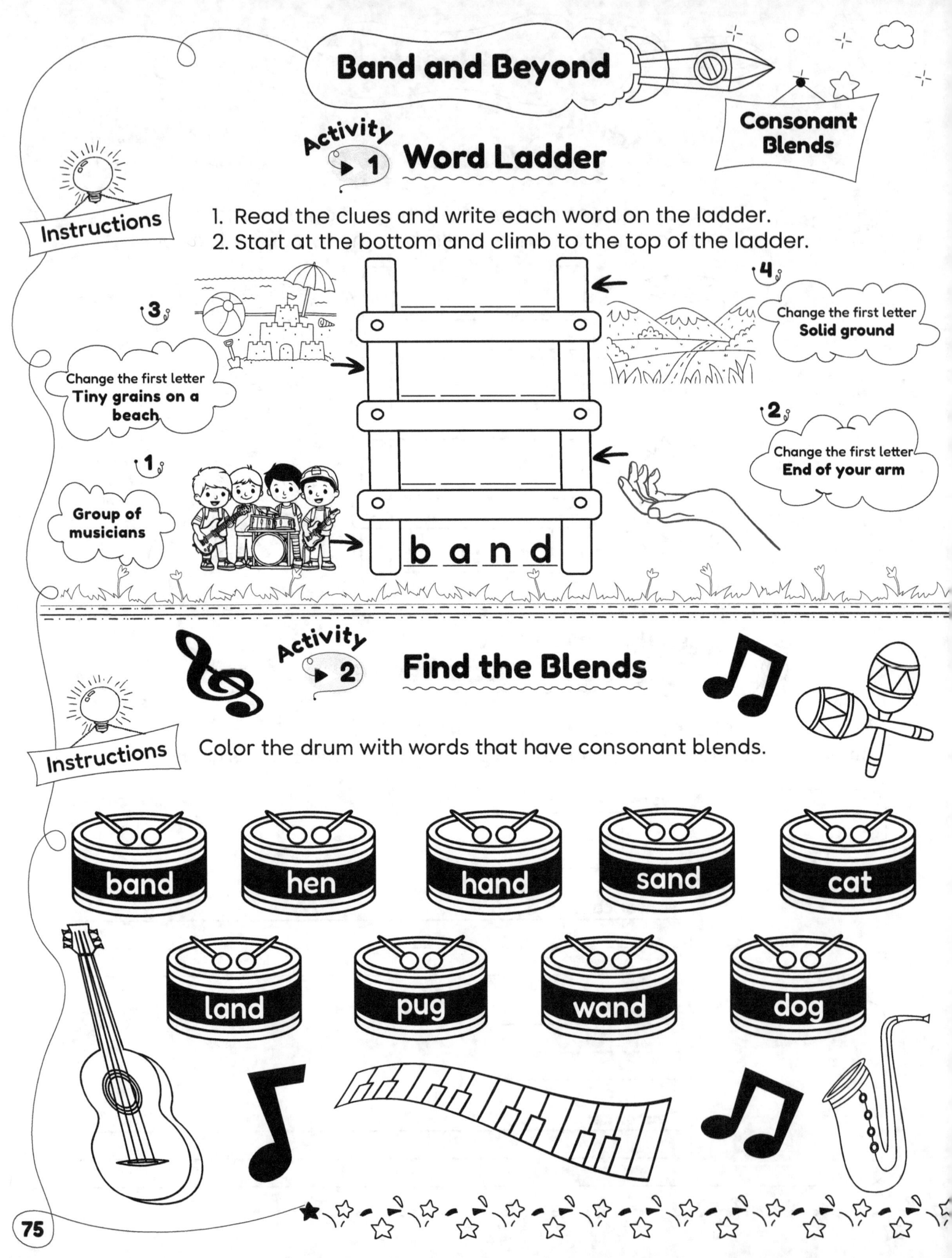

Crabby Claws

Activity 1 Word Ladder

Instructions

1. Read the clues and write each word on the ladder.
2. Start at the bottom and climb to the top of the ladder.

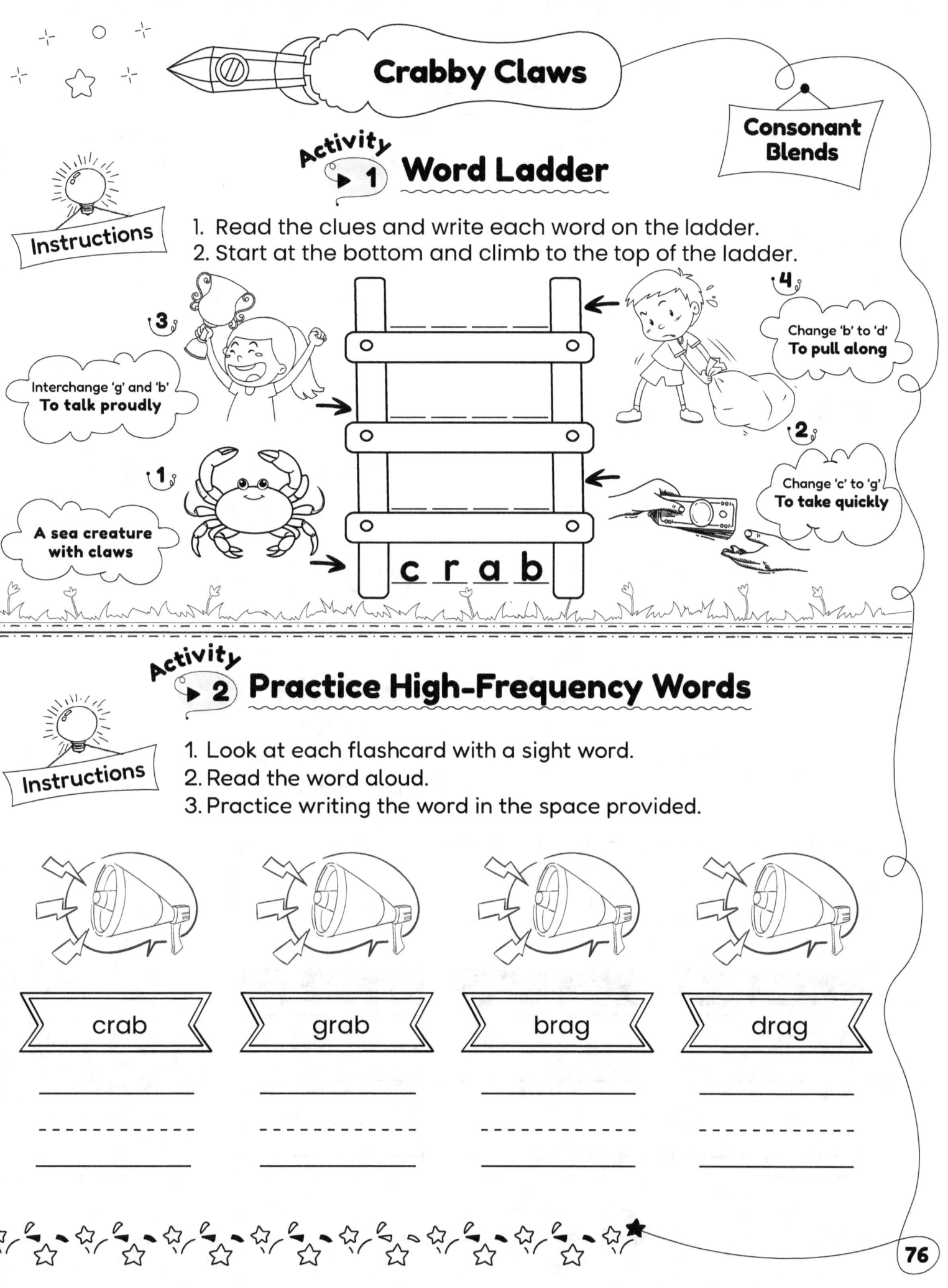

3 Interchange 'g' and 'b'
To talk proudly

1 A sea creature with claws

4 Change 'b' to 'd'
To pull along

2 Change 'c' to 'g'
To take quickly

c r a b

Activity 2 Practice High-Frequency Words

Instructions

1. Look at each flashcard with a sight word.
2. Read the word aloud.
3. Practice writing the word in the space provided.

crab   grab   brag   drag

76

Flipping Fun

Activity 1 Word Ladder

1. Read the clues and write each word on the ladder.
2. Start at the bottom and climb to the top of the ladder.

3 Change 'f' to 'c'
To hit your hands together

4 Change 'c' to 's'
To hit with an open hand

1 **To turn over quickly**

2 Change 'i' to 'a'
To move up and down

f l i p

Activity 2 Blend and Write

Write each word from the word bank in the correct column based on its consonant blend.

Word Bank

flap	slap	clap	flip

sl	cl	fl

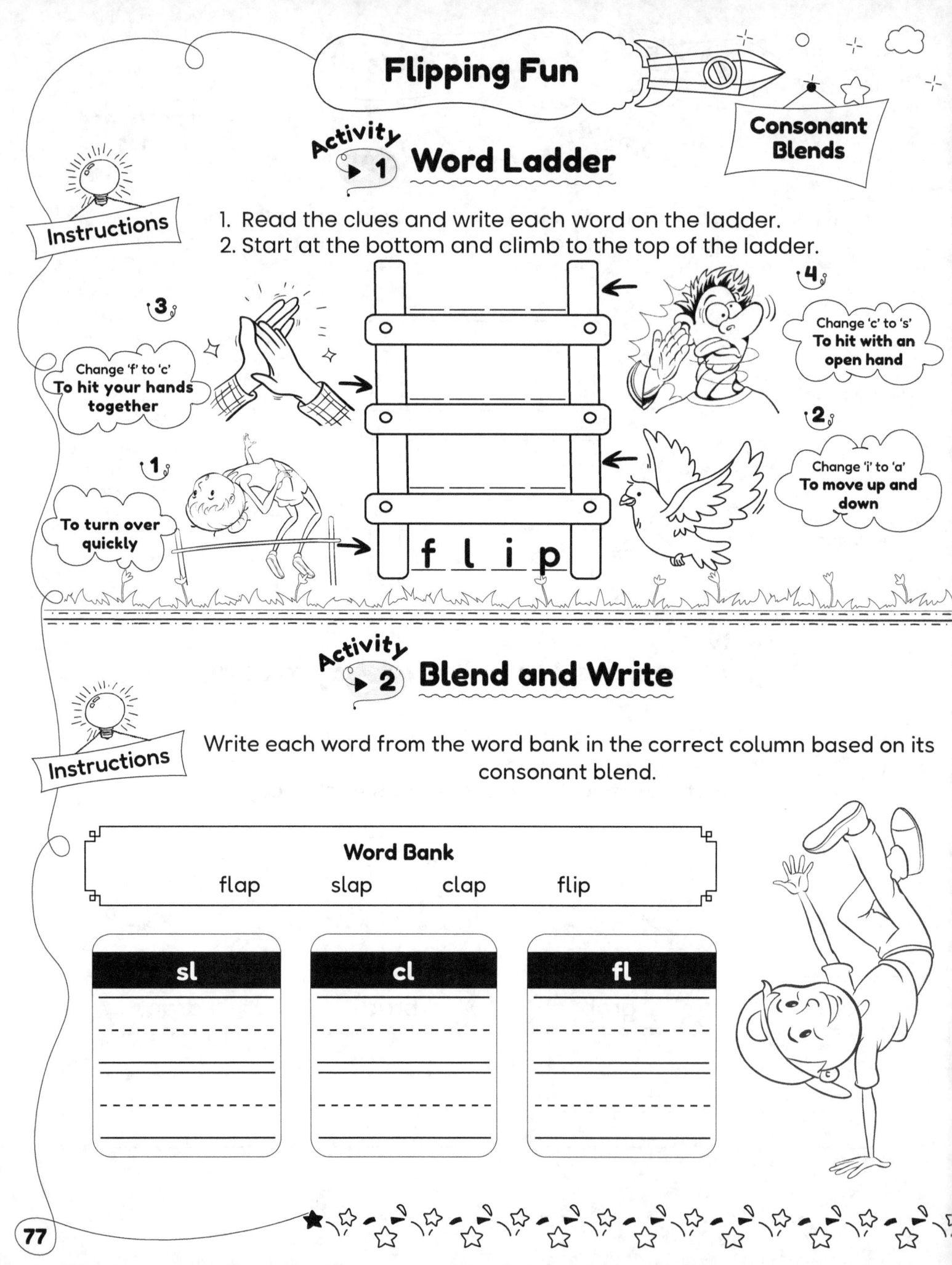

Spy Quest

Activity 1 Word Ladder

Instructions
1. Read the clues and write each word on the ladder.
2. Start at the bottom and climb to the top of the ladder.

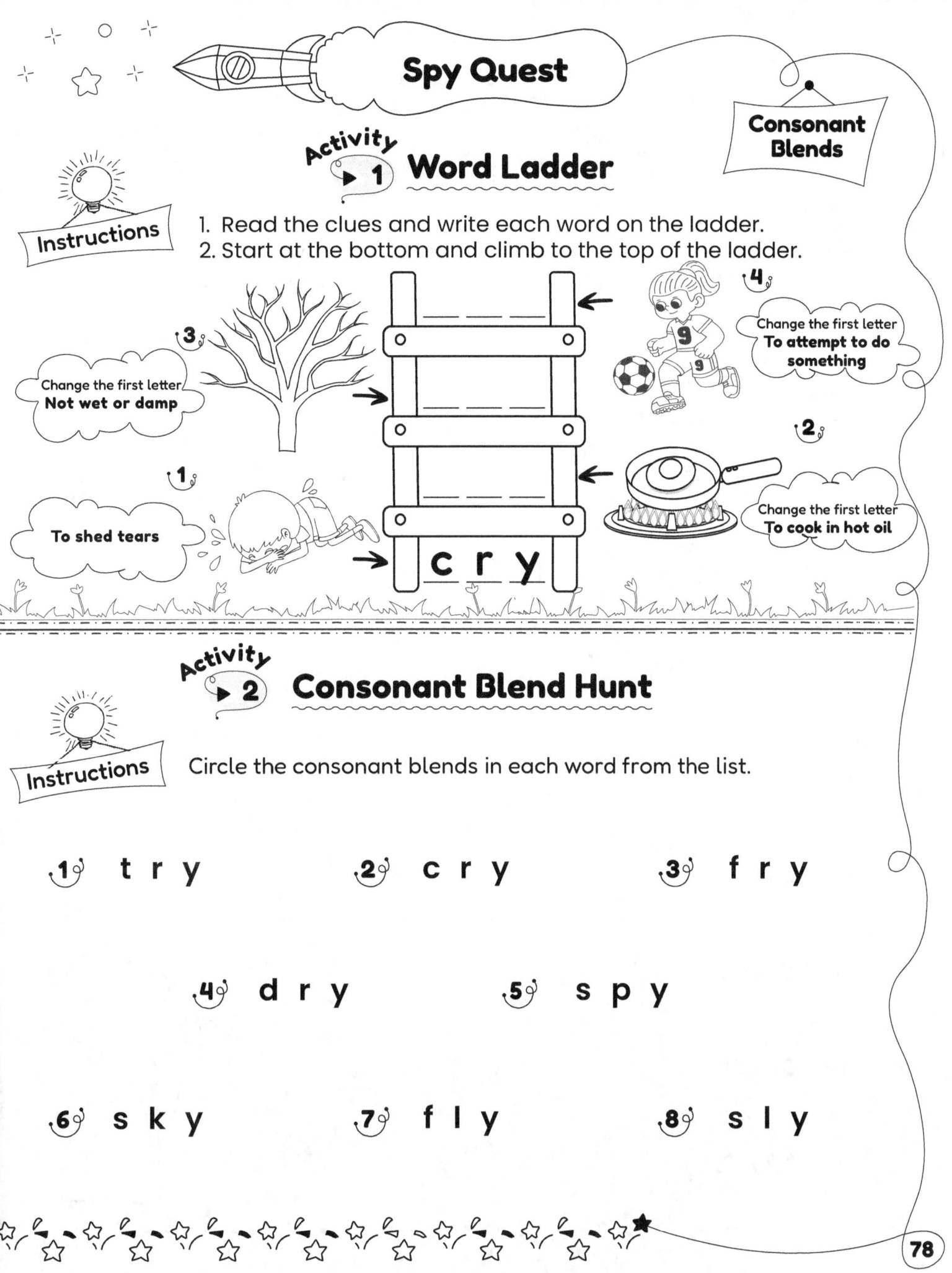

3 Change the first letter
Not wet or damp

1 To shed tears

4 Change the first letter
To attempt to do something

2 Change the first letter
To cook in hot oil

c r y

Activity 2 Consonant Blend Hunt

Instructions Circle the consonant blends in each word from the list.

1 t r y   **2** c r y   **3** f r y

4 d r y   **5** s p y

6 s k y   **7** f l y   **8** s l y

78

Blown Away

Activity 1 Word Ladder

Instructions

1. Read the clues and write each word on the ladder.
2. Start at the bottom and climb to the top of the ladder.

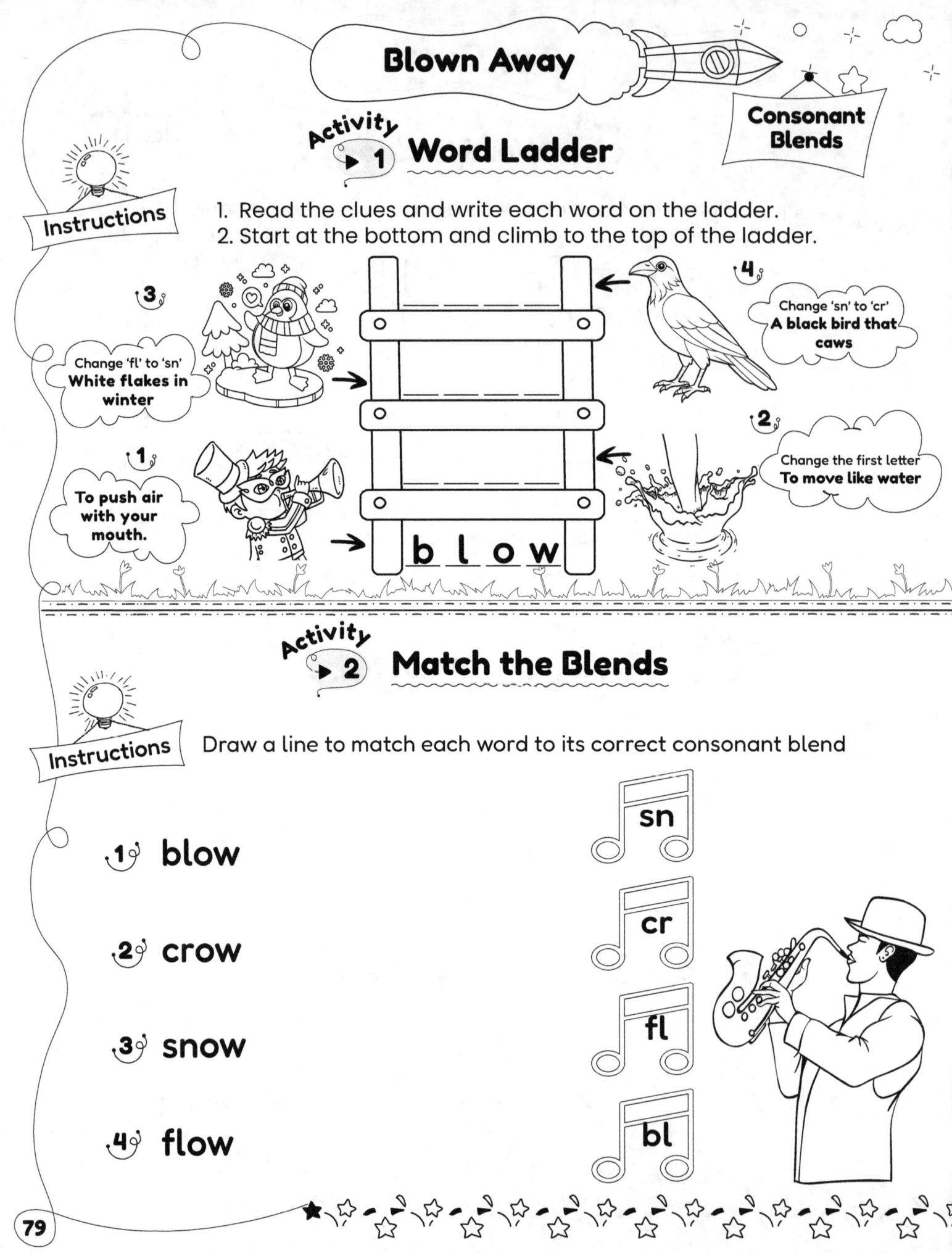

3 Change 'fl' to 'sn'
White flakes in winter

1 **To push air with your mouth.**

4 Change 'sn' to 'cr'
A black bird that caws

2 Change the first letter
To move like water

b l o w

Activity 2 Match the Blends

Instructions Draw a line to match each word to its correct consonant blend

1. blow
2. crow
3. snow
4. flow

sn

cr

fl

bl

Sail the Words

Digraphs

Activity 1 Word Ladder

Instructions

1. Read the clues and write each word on the ladder.
2. Start at the bottom and climb to the top of the ladder.

4 Change 'n' to 't'
The back part of an animal

3 Change 'm' to 'n'
A small metal spike

2 Change 's' to 'm'
Letters and packages

1 Catches wind on a boat

s a i l

Activity 2 Simple Word Search

Instructions

1. Find words from the word ladder within the grid.
2. Circle the words when you find them

M	B	V	W	N
V	A	O	A	T
S	A	I	L	A
Y	L	F	L	I
Y	F	U	L	L

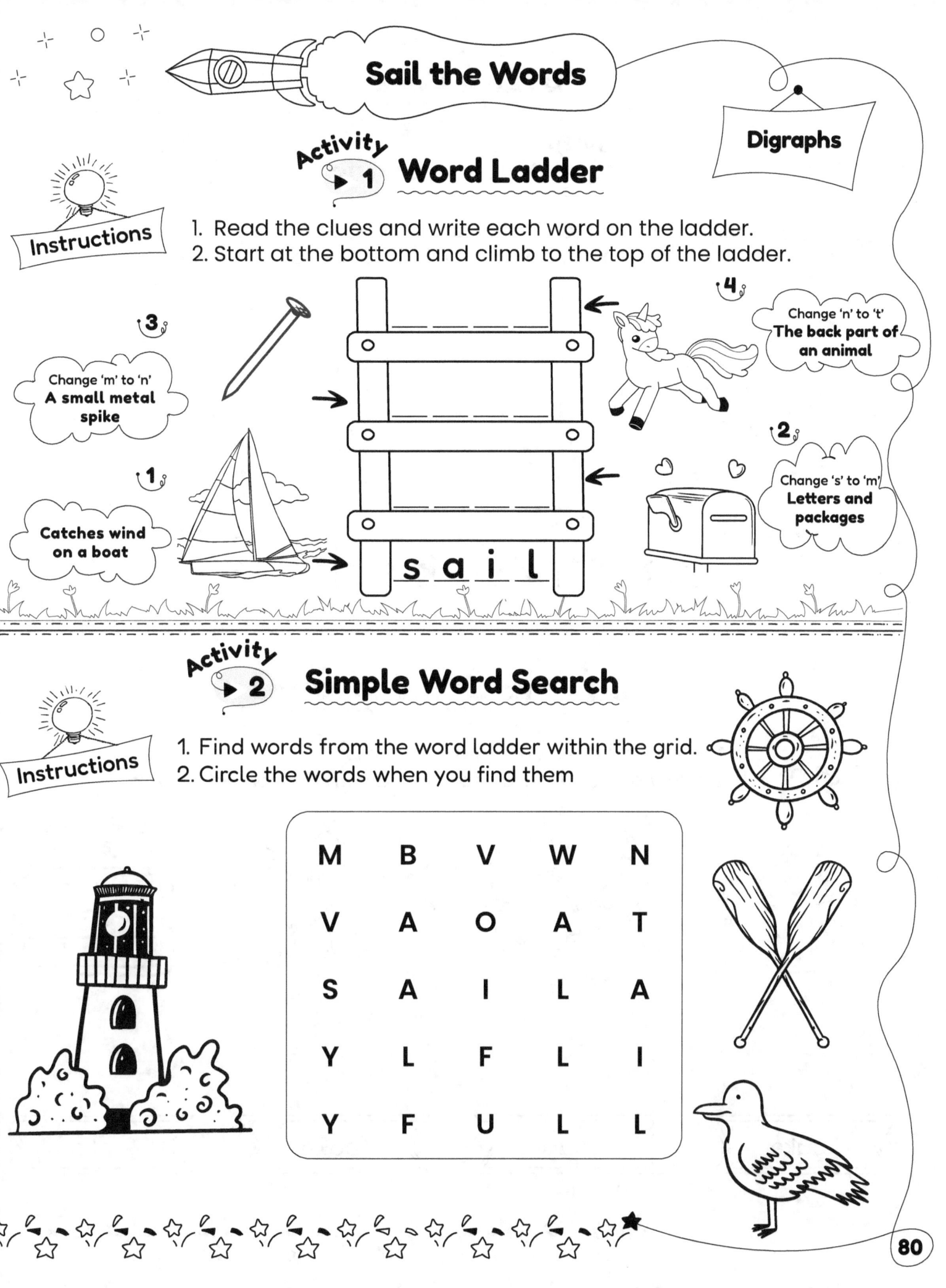

Bake a Cake

Activity ▶ 1 Word Ladder

1. Read the clues and write each word on the ladder.
2. Start at the bottom and climb to the top of the ladder.

3 Change the first letter
A body of water

4 Change the first letter
To create something

1 To cook in an oven

2 Change the first letter
A sweet dessert

b a k e

Activity ▶ 2 Match the Pictures

1. Look at the pictures and the words.
2. Draw a line to match each word with the correct picture.

bake   make   cake   lake

Dish Delights

Activity ▶ 1 Word Ladder

Instructions

1. Read the clues and write each word on the ladder.
2. Start at the bottom and climb to the top of the ladder.

3 Change 'd' to 'w'
To hope for

1 An animal in water

4 Add 's' at the beginning
A quick sound

2 Change 'f' to 'd'
A plate

f i s h

Activity ▶ 2 Fill in the Blanks

Instructions

1. Complete each sentence with a word from the word bank.
2. Write the word in the blank space.

1 The _____ swam gracefully in the water.

2 She placed the salad on a large _____ .

3 I _____ I could have a puppy for my birthday.

4 The ball went _____ in the hoop.

Word Bank

wish
swish
fish
dish

Math Adventure

Activity 1 — Word Ladder

1. Read the clues and write each word on the ladder.
2. Start at the bottom and climb to the top of the ladder.

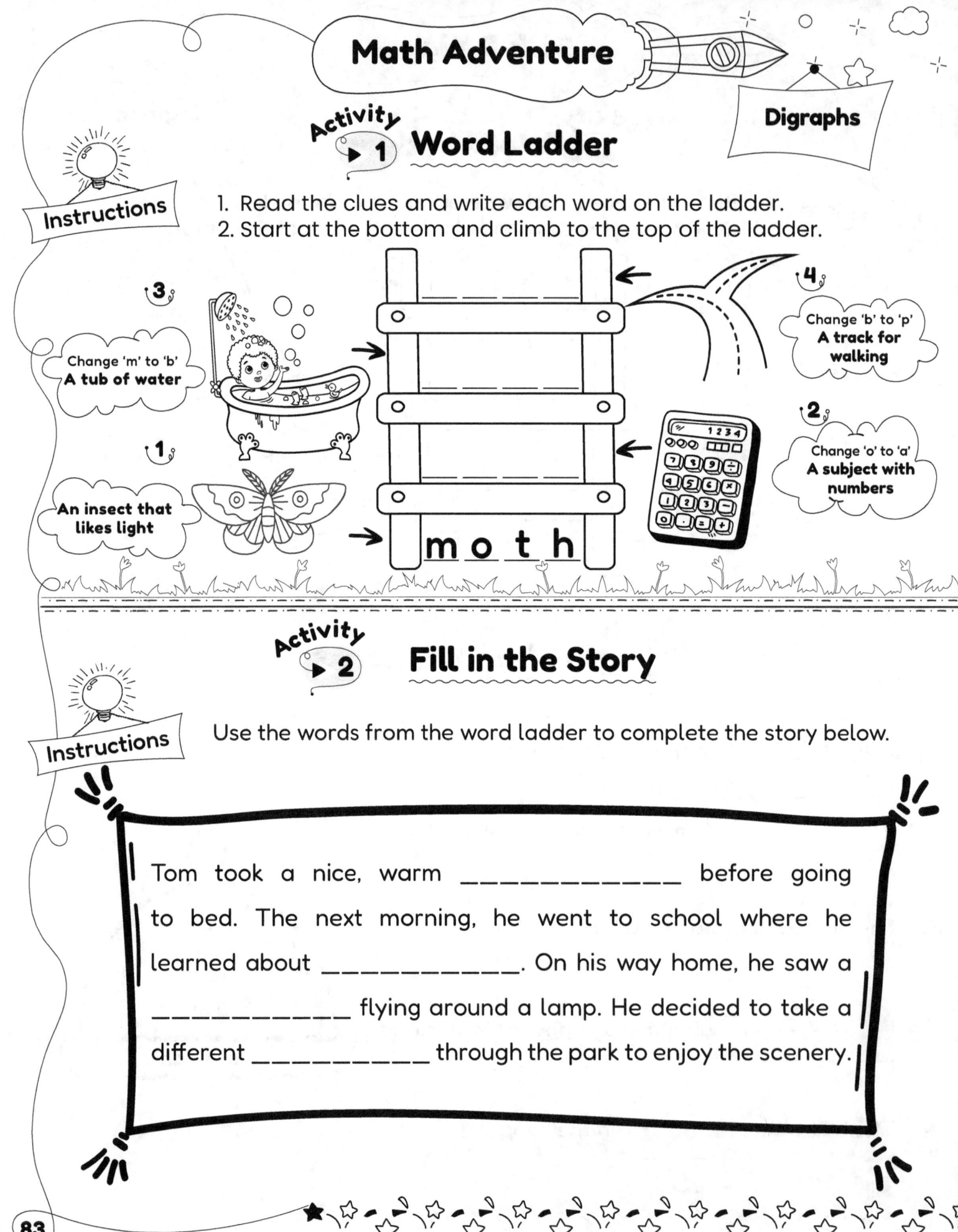

3 Change 'm' to 'b'
A tub of water

4 Change 'b' to 'p'
A track for walking

1 **An insect that likes light**

2 Change 'o' to 'a'
A subject with numbers

m o t h

Activity 2 — Fill in the Story

Use the words from the word ladder to complete the story below.

Tom took a nice, warm _____ before going to bed. The next morning, he went to school where he learned about _____. On his way home, he saw a _____ flying around a lamp. He decided to take a different _____ through the park to enjoy the scenery.

Chat with Chin

Activity 1 Word Ladder

Instructions

1. Read the clues and write each word on the ladder.
2. Start at the bottom and climb to the top of the ladder.

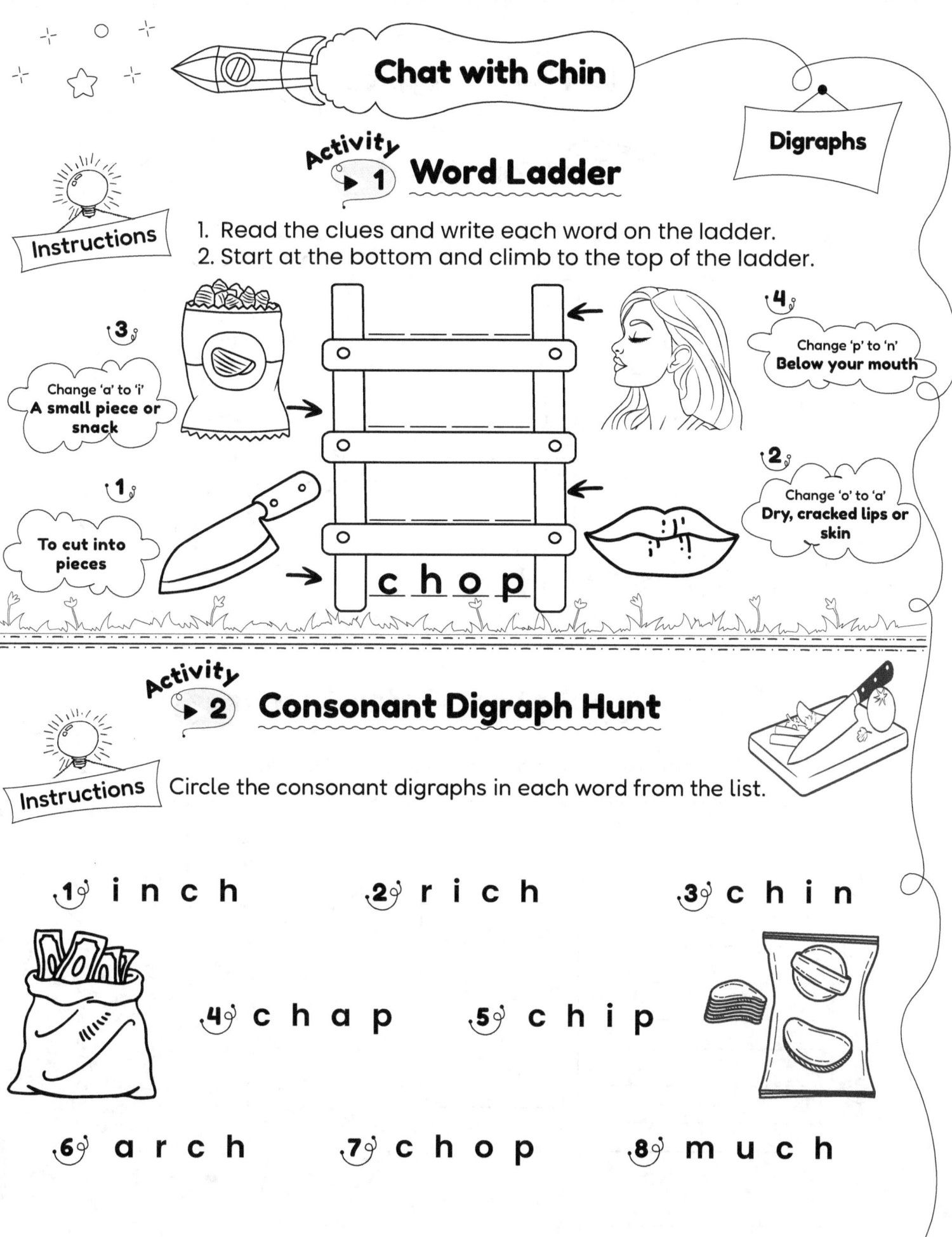

3 Change 'a' to 'i'
A small piece or snack

1 To cut into pieces

4 Change 'p' to 'n'
Below your mouth

2 Change 'o' to 'a'
Dry, cracked lips or skin

c h o p

Activity 2 Consonant Digraph Hunt

Instructions Circle the consonant digraphs in each word from the list.

1. i n c h   2. r i c h   3. c h i n

4. c h a p   5. c h i p

6. a r c h   7. c h o p   8. m u c h

Darting Delights

Activity 1 — Word Ladder

1. Read the clues and write each word on the ladder.
2. Start at the bottom and climb to the top of the ladder.

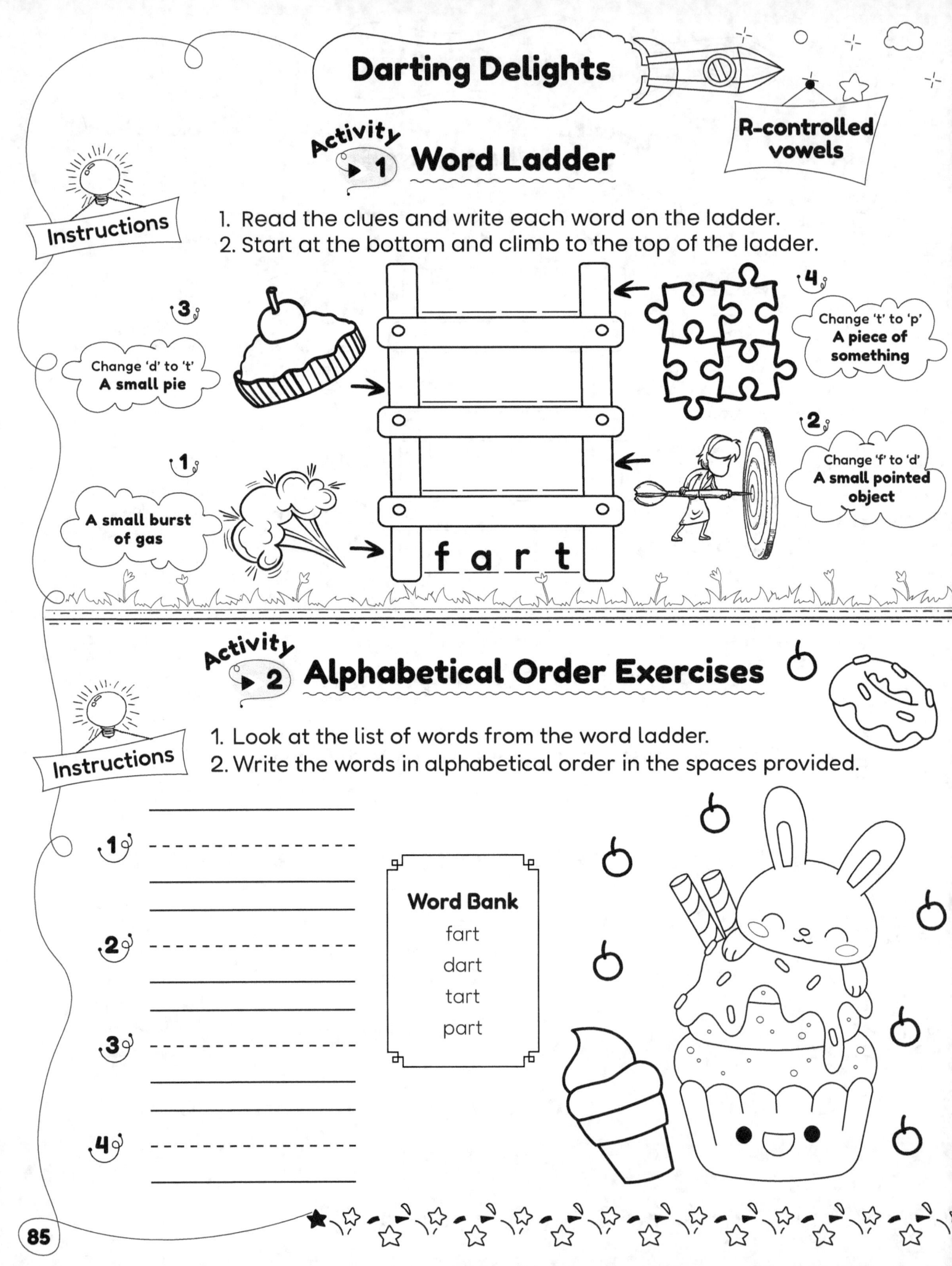

3 Change 'd' to 't'
A small pie

4 Change 't' to 'p'
A piece of something

1 **A small burst of gas**

2 Change 'f' to 'd'
A small pointed object

f a r t

Activity 2 — Alphabetical Order Exercises

1. Look at the list of words from the word ladder.
2. Write the words in alphabetical order in the spaces provided.

1 _____

2 _____

3 _____

4 _____

Word Bank
fart
dart
tart
part

Yarn Adventures

Activity ▶ 1 Word Ladder

Instructions

1. Read the clues and write each word on the ladder.
2. Start at the bottom and climb to the top of the ladder.

3 Change 'u' to 'a'
A building on a farm

4 Change 'b' to 'y'
A thread used for knitting

1 To move in a different direction

2 Change 't' to 'b'
To be on fire

t u r n

Activity ▶ 2 Draw and Write

Instructions

1. Choose two words from the word ladder.
2. Draw a picture for each word and write a sentence using that word.

1

Word: _____ _____ _____

Sentence: _____

2

Word: _____ _____ _____

Sentence: _____

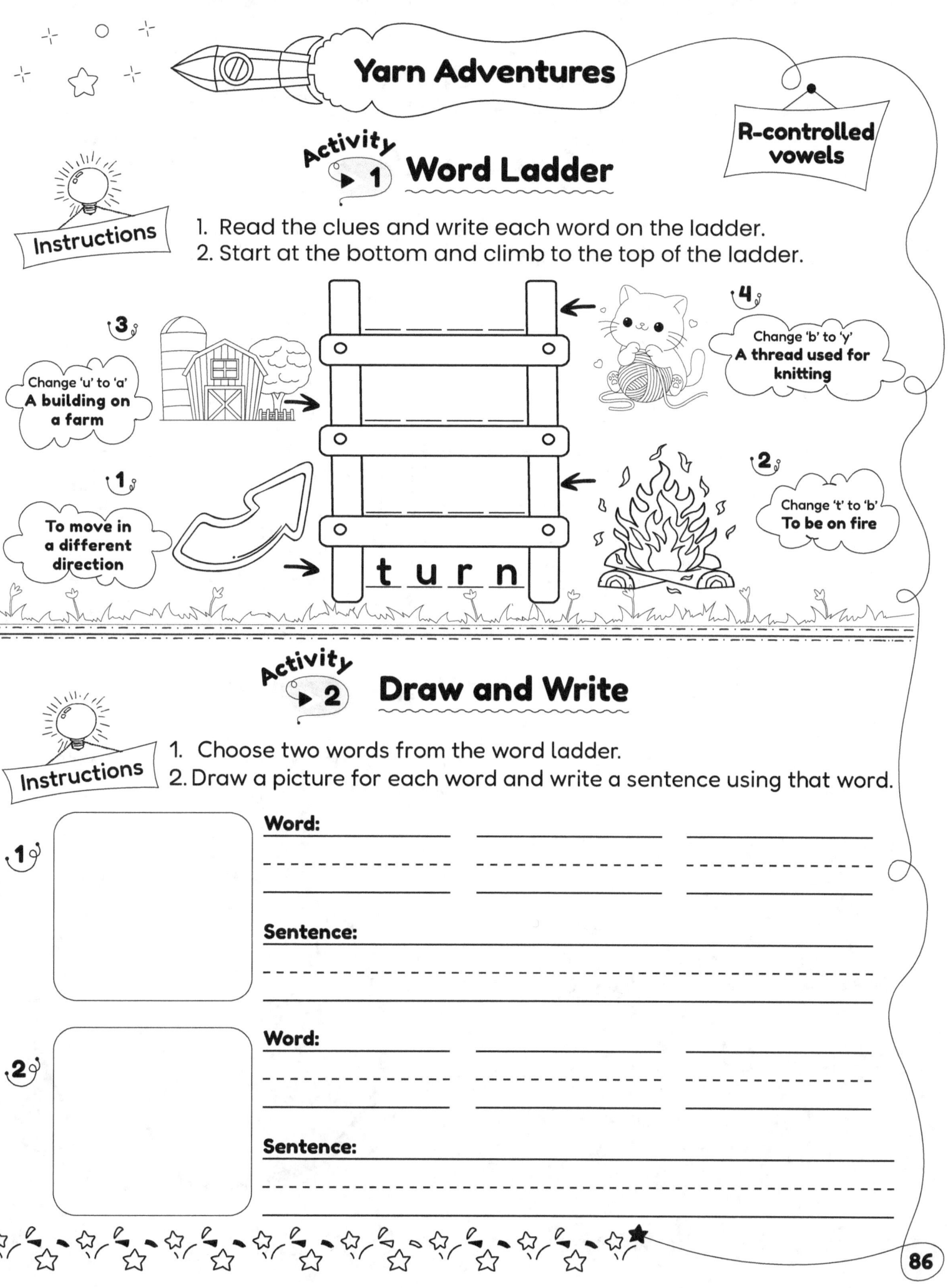

Curly Craze

Activity 1 Word Ladder

R-controlled vowels

Instructions

1. Read the clues and write each word on the ladder.
2. Start at the bottom and climb to the top of the ladder.

3 Change 'u' to 'a'
A piece of thick paper

4 Change 'd' to 't'
A vehicle with wheels

1 To form a spiral shape

2 Change 'l' to 'd'
A thickened part of milk

Milk

c u r l

Activity 2 Rhyming Words Activity

Instructions

Draw a picture of your favorite word that has R-controlled vowels -ar and -ur .

curl

_____
- - - - - - - -

Activity 1 Word Ladder

Instructions

1. Read the clues and write each word on the ladder.
2. Start at the bottom and climb to the top of the ladder.

3 Change 'b' to 'd'
Having little or no light

4 Change 'd' to 'm'
A small area or spot

1 **A place with grass and trees**

2 Change 'p' to 'b'
The sound a dog makes

p a r k

Activity 2 Sentence Scramble

Instructions

1. Unscramble the words to form correct sentences.
2. Write the sentences on the lines provided.

1 dog The bark likes to.

2 room The dark is at night.

3 left He mark a on the paper.

4 played They in the park.

Horn Born Journey

R-controlled vowels

Activity 1 Word Ladder

Instructions

1. Read the clues and write each word on the ladder.
2. Start at the bottom and climb to the top of the ladder.

3. Change 'c' to 'b'
To come into the world

4. Change 'b' to 'r'
Ripped

1. **A hard, pointed part on an animal.**

2. Change 'h' to 'c'
A type of grain

h o r n

Activity 2 Color by Code

Instructions

Color the words according to the code. Each color corresponds to a type of word.

Color Code
Red: Words with r-controlled vowels
Blue: Words with consonant blends
Green: Words with digraphs

horn

chat

born

dish

snow

corn

clap

89

Activity 1 Word Ladder

Instructions

1. Read the clues and write each word on the ladder.
2. Start at the bottom and climb to the top of the ladder.

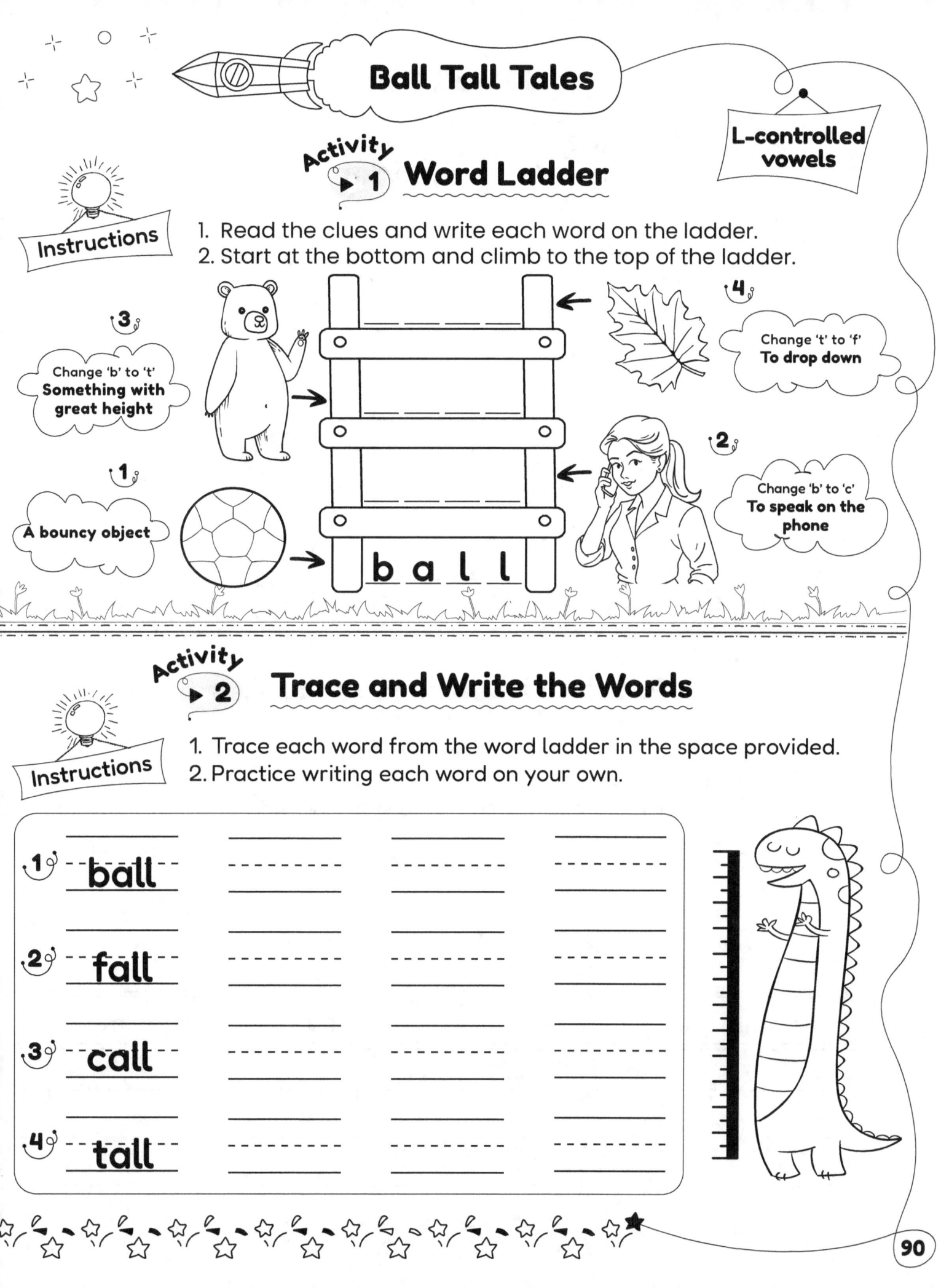

3 Change 'b' to 't'
Something with great height

4 Change 't' to 'f'
To drop down

1 **A bouncy object**

2 Change 'b' to 'c'
To speak on the phone

b a l l

Activity 2 Trace and Write the Words

Instructions

1. Trace each word from the word ladder in the space provided.
2. Practice writing each word on your own.

1. ball

2. fall

3. call

4. tall

Mall Wall Fun

Activity 1 — Word Ladder

Instructions

1. Read the clues and write each word on the ladder.
2. Start at the bottom and climb to the top of the ladder.

3 Add 's' at the beginning
Not large in size

1 **A solid divider**

4 Change 'm' to 't'
A small shop or booth

2 Change 'd' to 'm'
A large shopping center

w a l l

Activity 2 — Practice High-Frequency Words

Instructions

1. Look at each flashcard with a sight word.
2. Read the word aloud.
3. Practice writing the word in the space provided.

mall

wall

stall

small

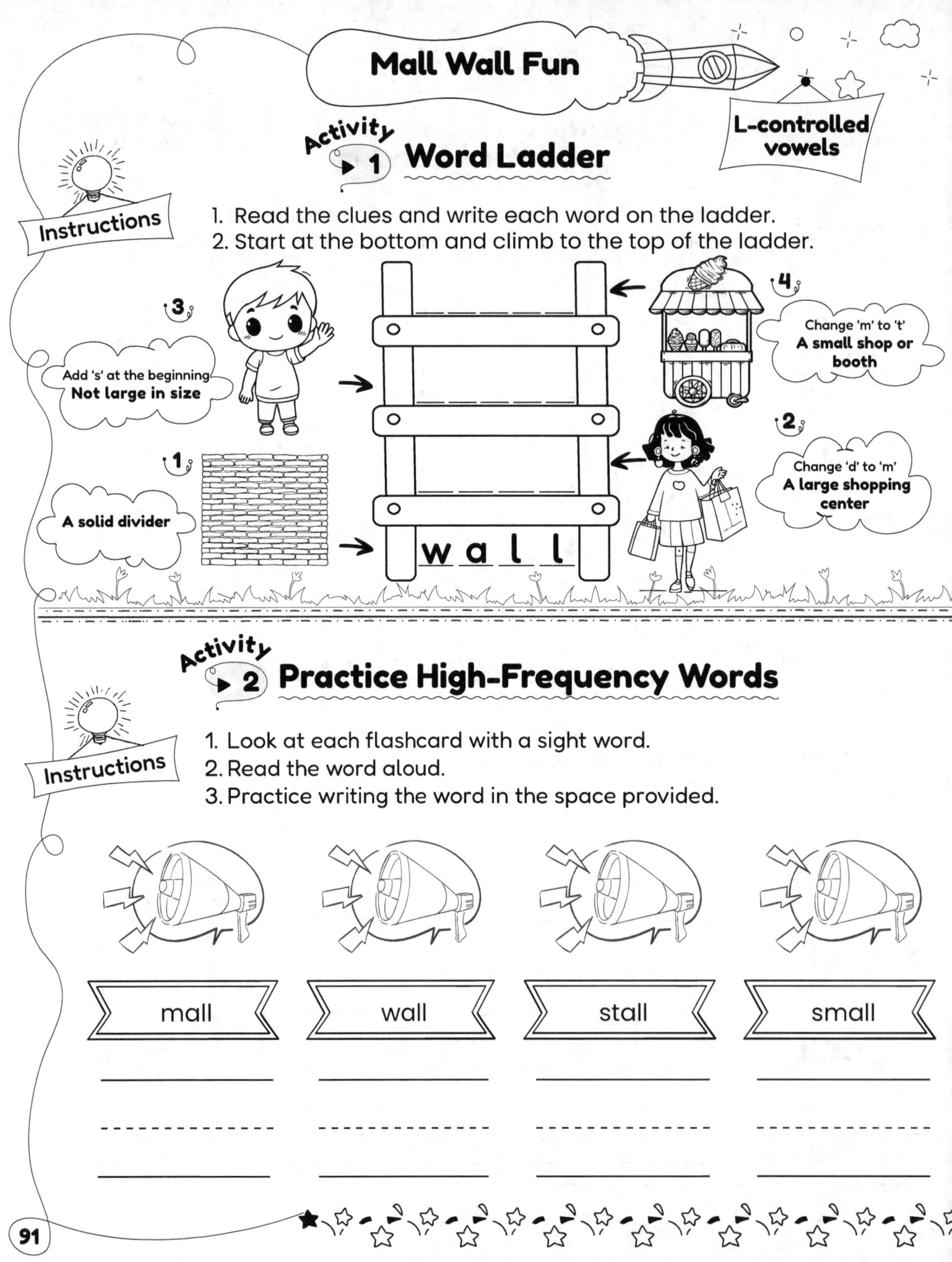

Activity 1 — Word Ladder

Instructions

1. Read the clues and write each word on the ladder.
2. Start at the bottom and climb to the top of the ladder.

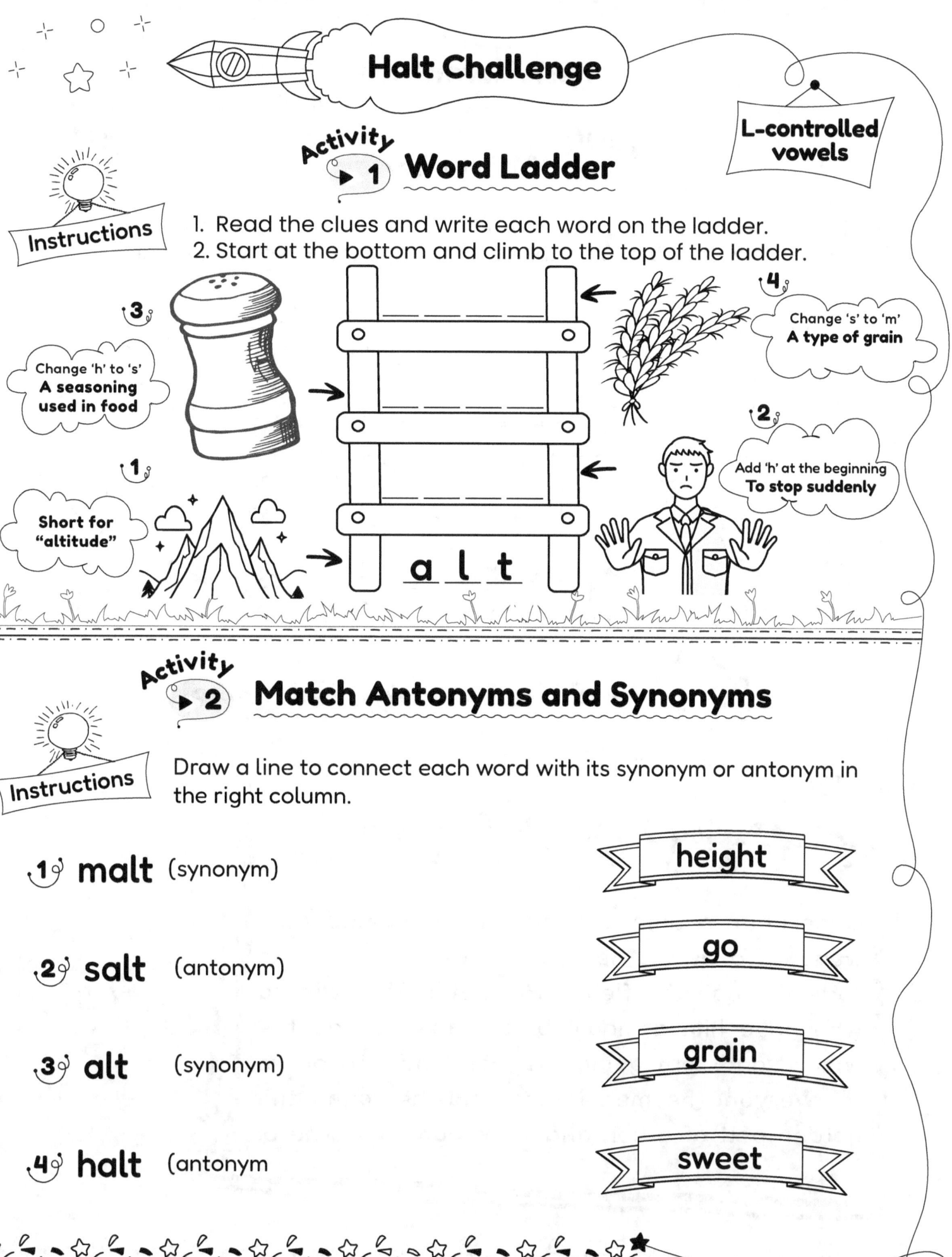

3 Change 'h' to 's'
A seasoning used in food

4 Change 's' to 'm'
A type of grain

2 Add 'h' at the beginning
To stop suddenly

1 Short for "altitude"

a l t

Activity 2 — Match Antonyms and Synonyms

Instructions

Draw a line to connect each word with its synonym or antonym in the right column.

1 malt (synonym)

2 salt (antonym)

3 alt (synonym)

4 halt (antonym

height

go

grain

sweet

Felt Adventure

L-controlled vowels

Activity 1 Word Ladder

Instructions

1. Read the clues and write each word on the ladder.
2. Start at the bottom and climb to the top of the ladder.

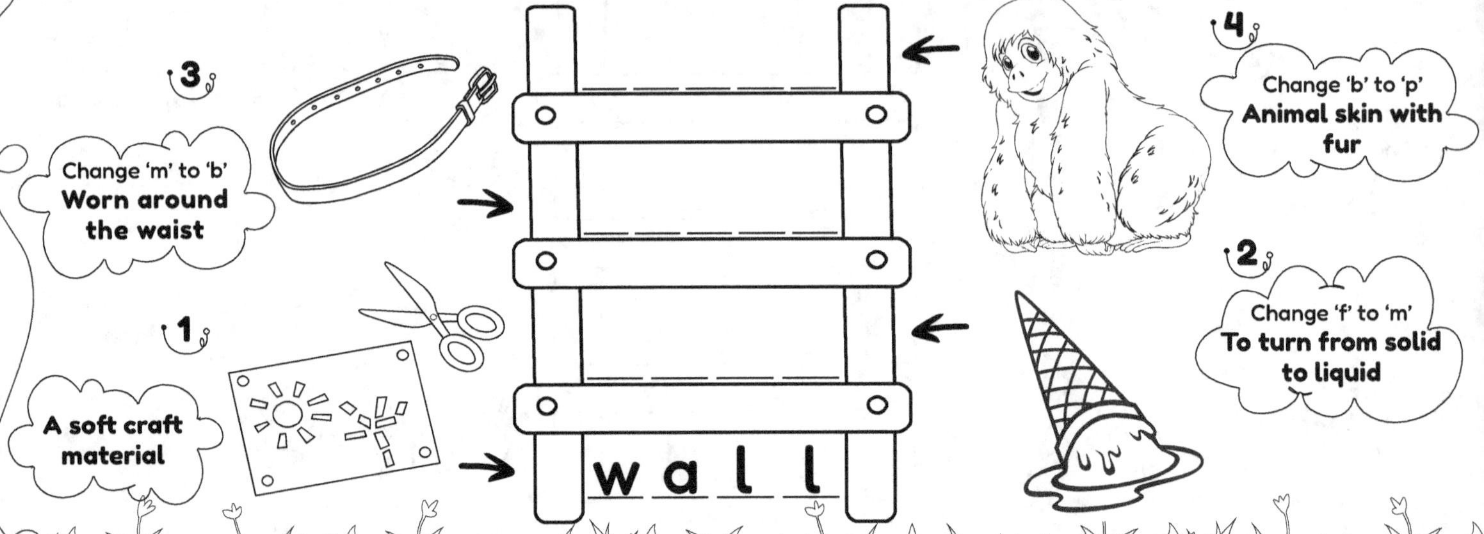

4
Change 'b' to 'p'
Animal skin with fur
3
Change 'm' to 'b'
Worn around the waist
2
Change 'f' to 'm'
To turn from solid to liquid
1
A soft craft material
w a l l

Activity 2 Find the L-Controlled Vowels

Instructions

Encircle all the words that have L-controlled vowels.

Once upon a time, a brave knight named Alex went on a quest. He felt the warm sun as he rode through the fields. He met a kind wizard who gave him a magic belt. Alex thanked the wizard and kept going. He was kind and brave to everyone he met. In the end, he found the golden pelt of a lion and went home as a hero.

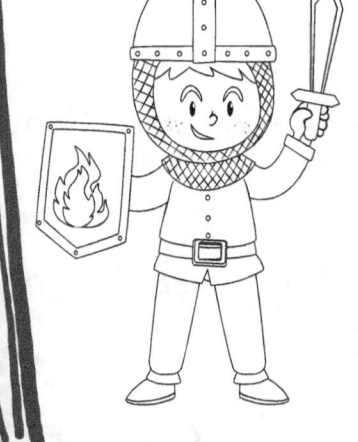

Gold Escapades

L-controlled vowels

Activity 1 Word Ladder

Instructions

1. Read the clues and write each word on the ladder.
2. Start at the bottom and climb to the top of the ladder.

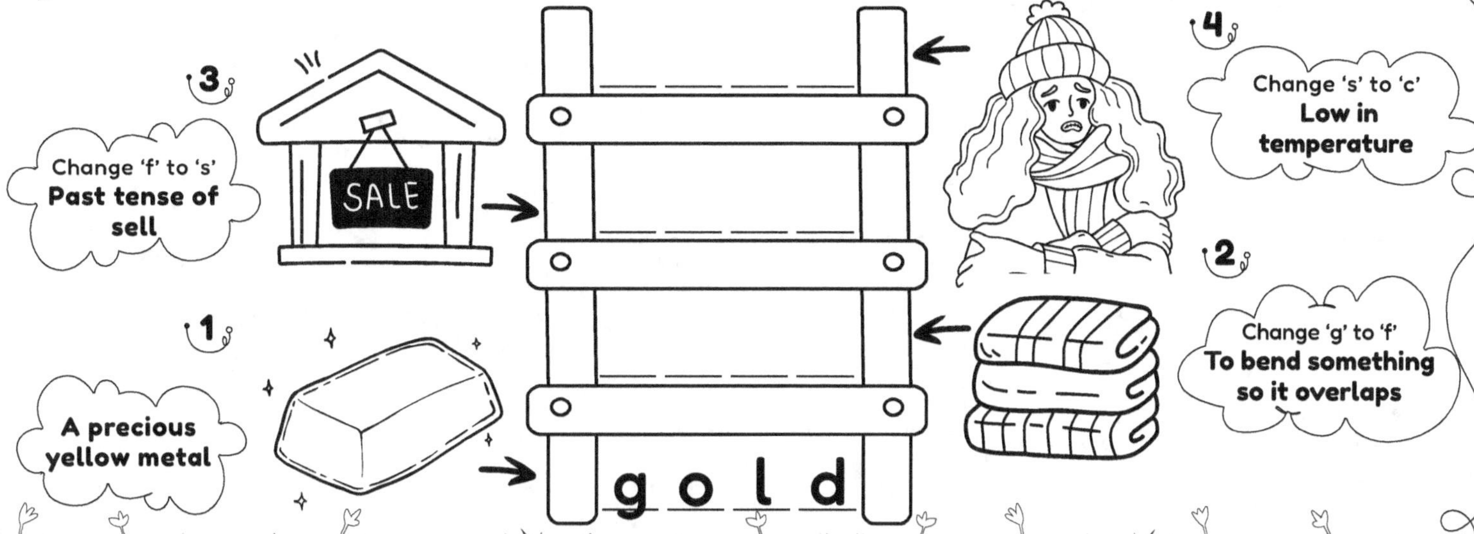

4
Change 's' to 'c'
Low in temperature
3
Change 'f' to 's'
Past tense of sell
SALE
2
Change 'g' to 'f'
To bend something so it overlaps
1
A precious yellow metal
g o l d

Activity 2 Story Time

Instructions

1. Read the short story. Then, answer the questions below.
2. Write your answer on the space provided.

Tom found gold while digging in his backyard. He showed it to his friend. They folded their map and decided to explore more. They sold some gold and bought ice cream. It was a cold but exciting day.

1. What did Tom find in his backyard? ______________________

2. How was the weather that day? ______________________

Paw Patrol

-aw

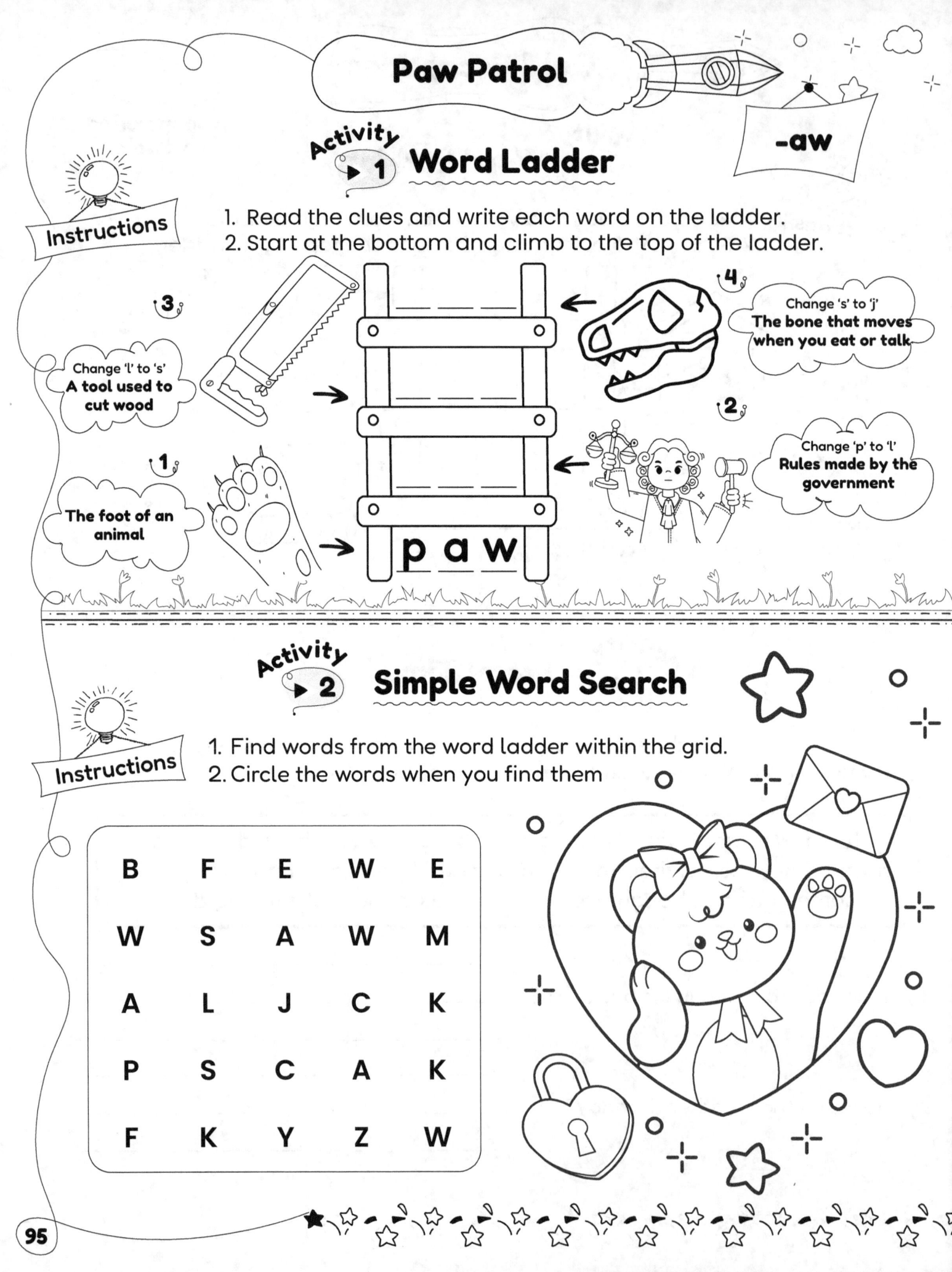

Activity ▶ 1 Word Ladder

Instructions

1. Read the clues and write each word on the ladder.
2. Start at the bottom and climb to the top of the ladder.

3 Change 'l' to 's'
A tool used to cut wood

4 Change 's' to 'j'
The bone that moves when you eat or talk

1 The foot of an animal

2 Change 'p' to 'l'
Rules made by the government

p a w

Activity ▶ 2 Simple Word Search

Instructions

1. Find words from the word ladder within the grid.
2. Circle the words when you find them

B	F	E	W	E
W	S	A	W	M
A	L	J	C	K
P	S	C	A	K
F	K	Y	Z	W

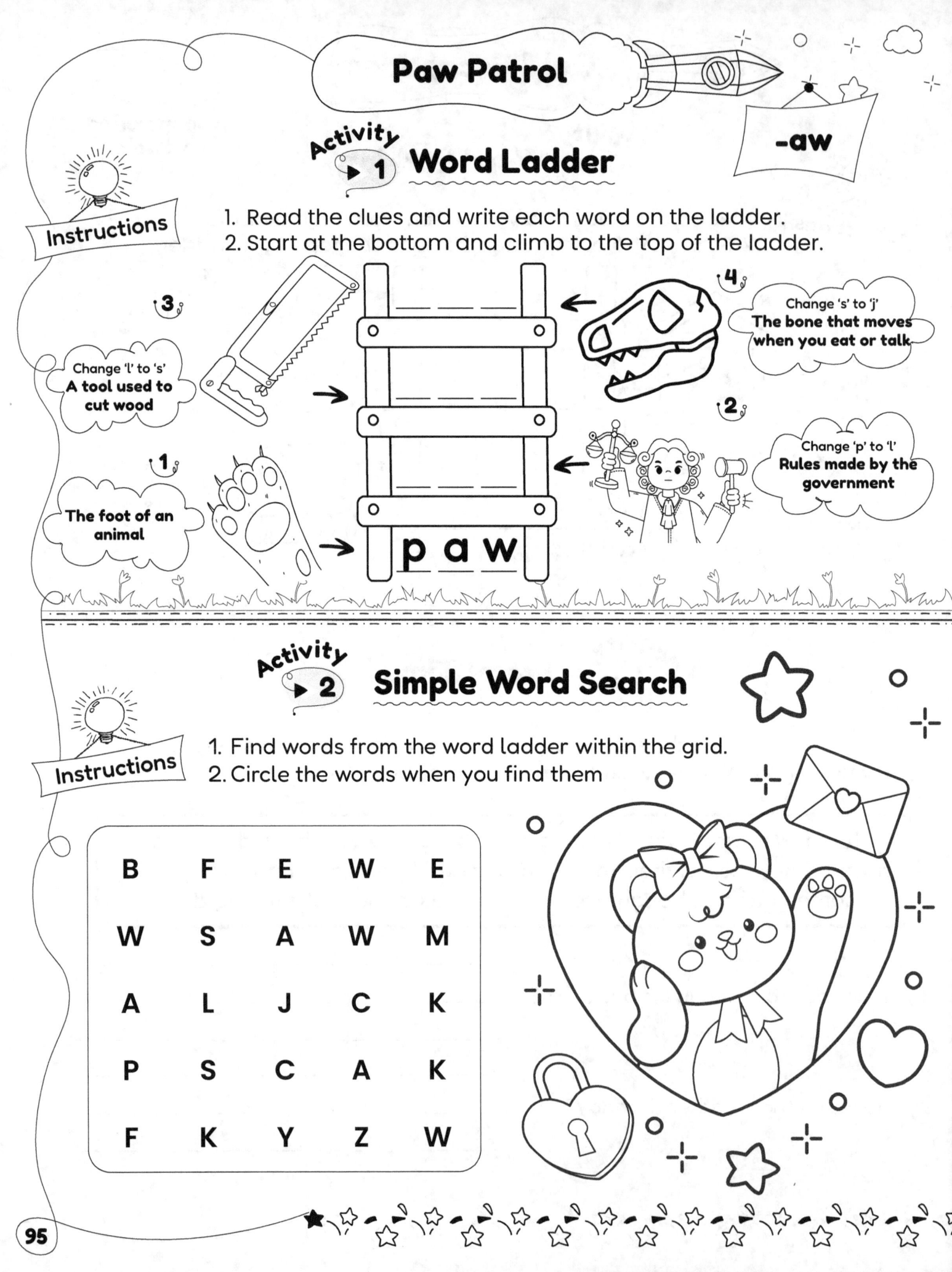

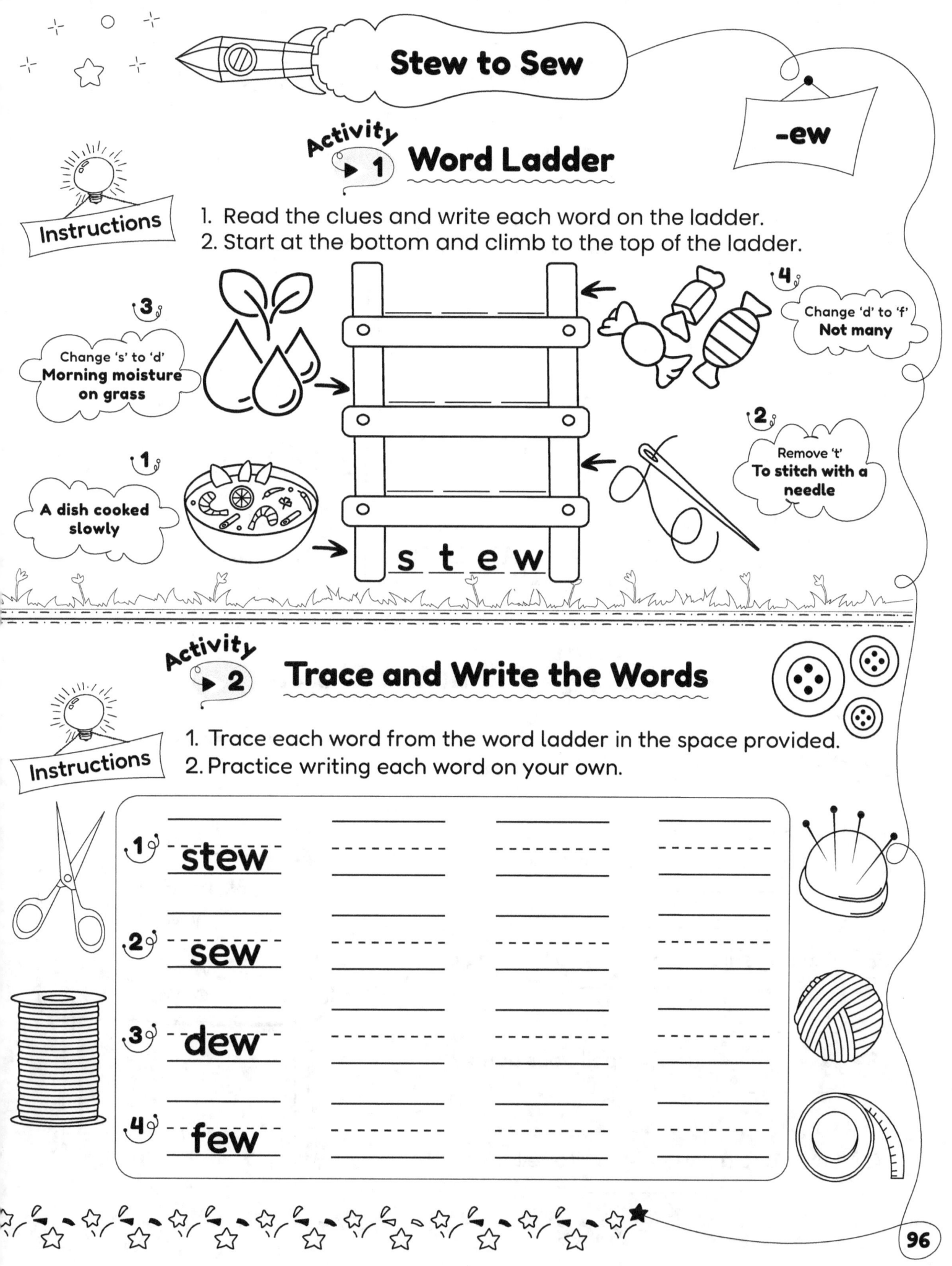

Stew to Sew

-ew

Activity 1 — Word Ladder

Instructions

1. Read the clues and write each word on the ladder.
2. Start at the bottom and climb to the top of the ladder.

3 Change 's' to 'd'
Morning moisture on grass

4 Change 'd' to 'f'
Not many

1 A dish cooked slowly

2 Remove 't'
To stitch with a needle

s t e w

Activity 2 — Trace and Write the Words

Instructions

1. Trace each word from the word ladder in the space provided.
2. Practice writing each word on your own.

1 stew

2 sew

3 dew

4 few

Cow's Adventure

-ow/ -oh

Activity ▶ 1 Word Ladder

Instructions

1. Read the clues and write each word on the ladder.
2. Start at the bottom and climb to the top of the ladder.

3. Change 'b' to 'h'
In what way

4. Change 'h' to 'v'
A serious promise

1. **An animal that gives milk**

2. Change 'c' to 'w'
You say it when you're surprised

C O W

Activity ▶ 2 Fill in the Blanks

Instructions

1. Choose the correct word below to complete each sentence.
2. Write the word in the blank space.

1. The _____ gives us milk.

2. The boy said _____ to the magician.

3. _____ do you spell your name?

4. She made a _____ to tell the truth.

Word Bank
how
vow
wow
cow

Shout It Out

Activity ▶ 1 Word Ladder

Instructions

1. Read the clues and write each word on the ladder.
2. Start at the bottom and climb to the top of the ladder.

3 Change 'p' to 'l' and 't' to 'd'
A lot of noise

4 Change 'l' to 'sh' and 'd' to 't'
To yell

1 **Not in**

2 Add 'p' at the beginning
To frown

o u t

Activity ▶ 2 Rhyming Words Activity

Instructions

Draw a picture of your favorite word that rhymes with 'shout'.

shout

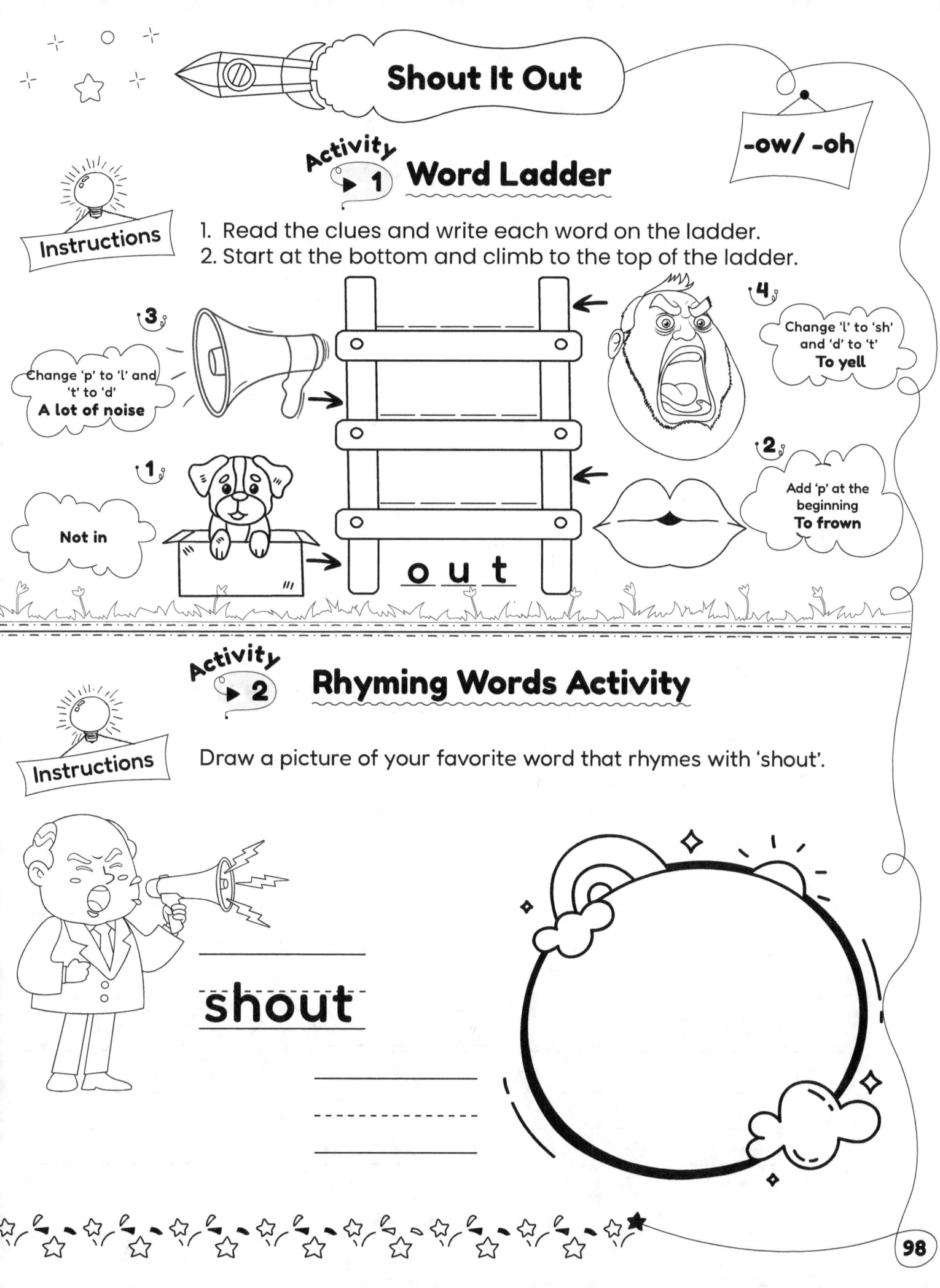

Boil the Coil

-oi

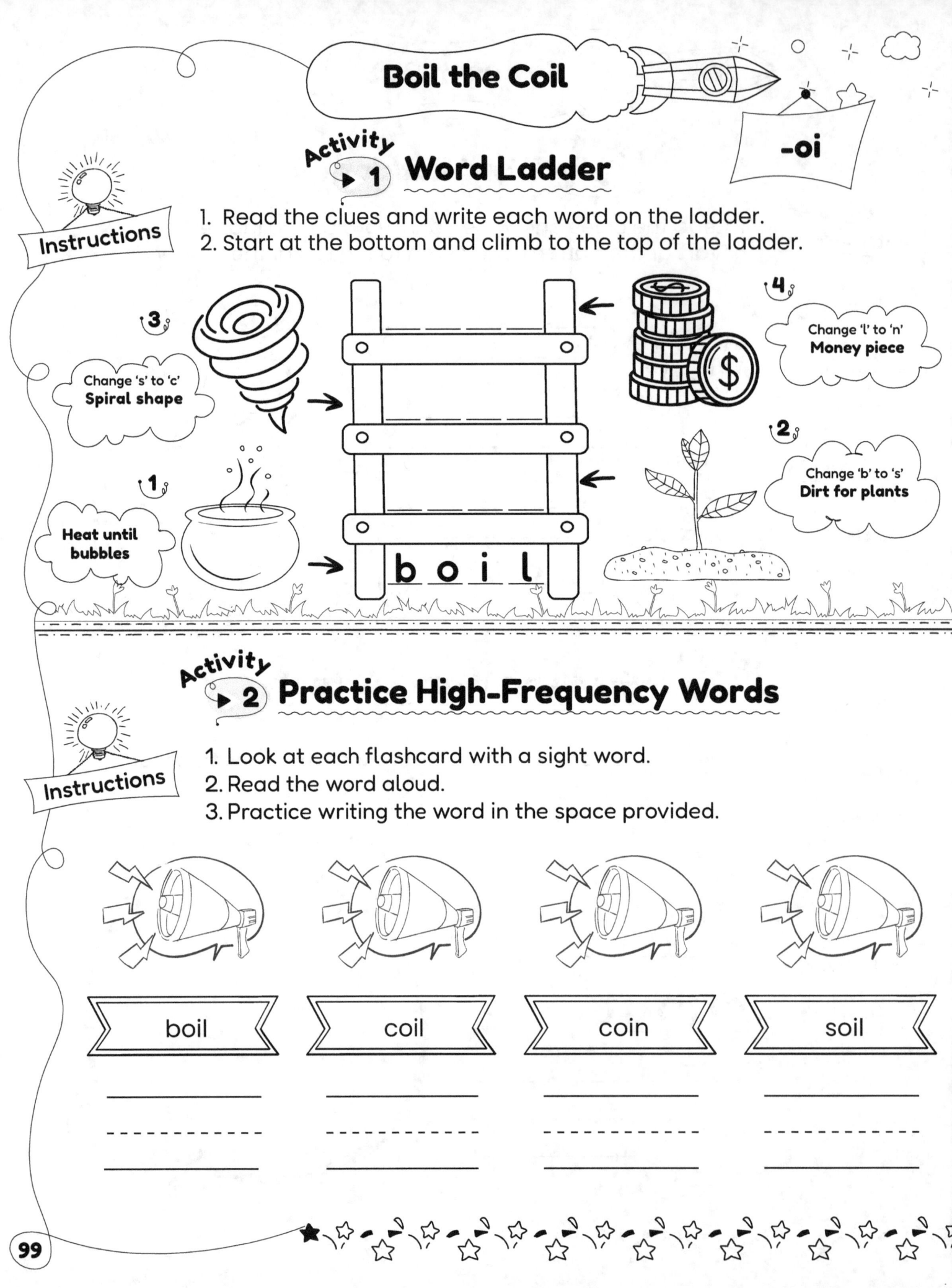

Activity 1 Word Ladder

Instructions
1. Read the clues and write each word on the ladder.
2. Start at the bottom and climb to the top of the ladder.

4 Change 'l' to 'n'
Money piece

3 Change 's' to 'c'
Spiral shape

2 Change 'b' to 's'
Dirt for plants

1 Heat until bubbles

b o i l

Activity 2 Practice High-Frequency Words

Instructions
1. Look at each flashcard with a sight word.
2. Read the word aloud.
3. Practice writing the word in the space provided.

boil	coil	coin	soil

99

Joyful Boy

Activity 1 — Word Ladder

Instructions

1. Read the clues and write each word on the ladder.
2. Start at the bottom and climb to the top of the ladder.

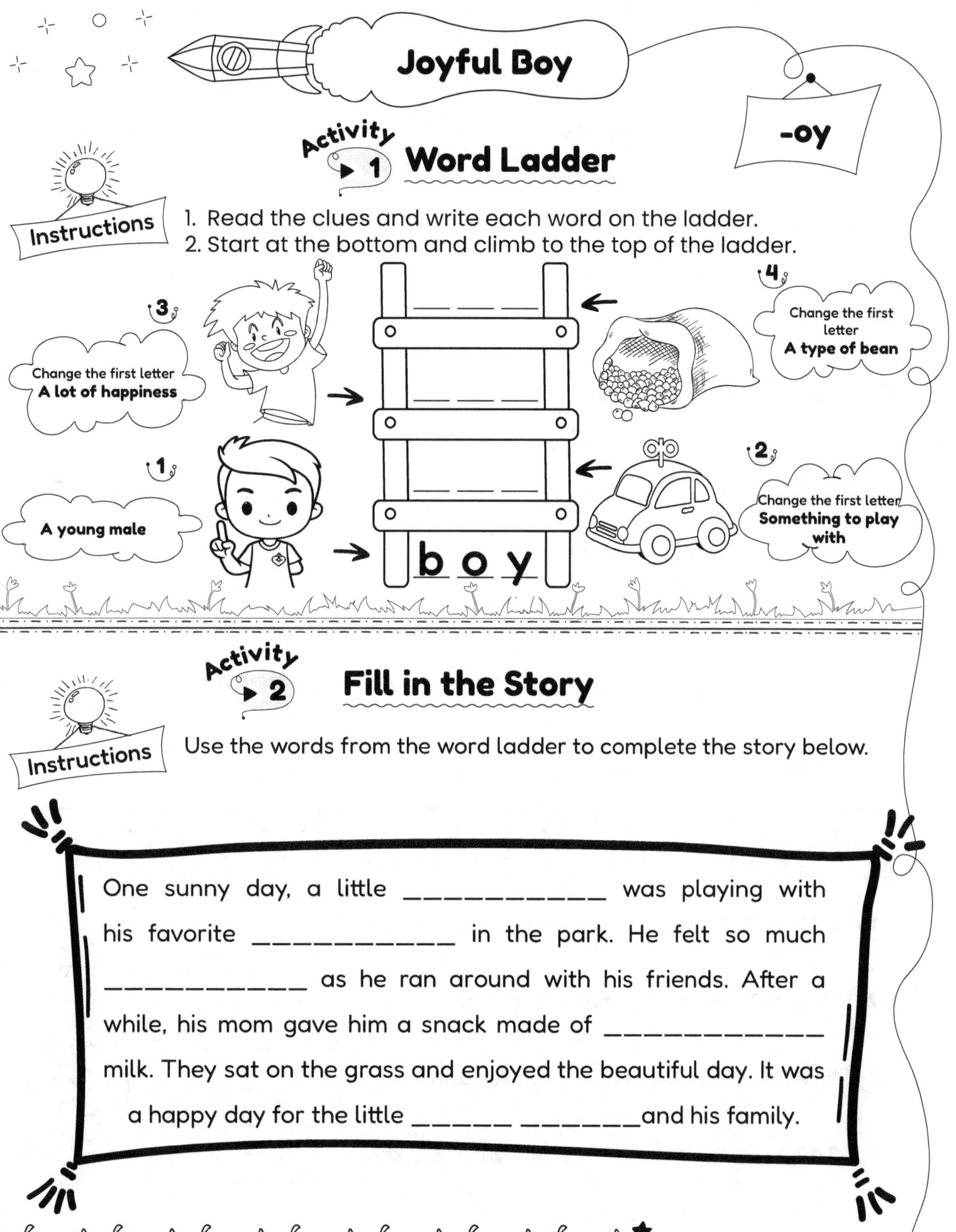

3 Change the first letter
A lot of happiness

4 Change the first letter
A type of bean

1 **A young male**

2 Change the first letter
Something to play with

b o y

Activity 2 — Fill in the Story

Instructions

Use the words from the word ladder to complete the story below.

One sunny day, a little _____ was playing with his favorite _____ in the park. He felt so much _____ as he ran around with his friends. After a while, his mom gave him a snack made of _____ milk. They sat on the grass and enjoyed the beautiful day. It was a happy day for the little _____ _____ and his family.

Straw Draw

Activity 1 — Word Ladder

-aw

Instructions

1. Read the clues and write each word on the ladder.
2. Start at the bottom and climb to the top of the ladder.

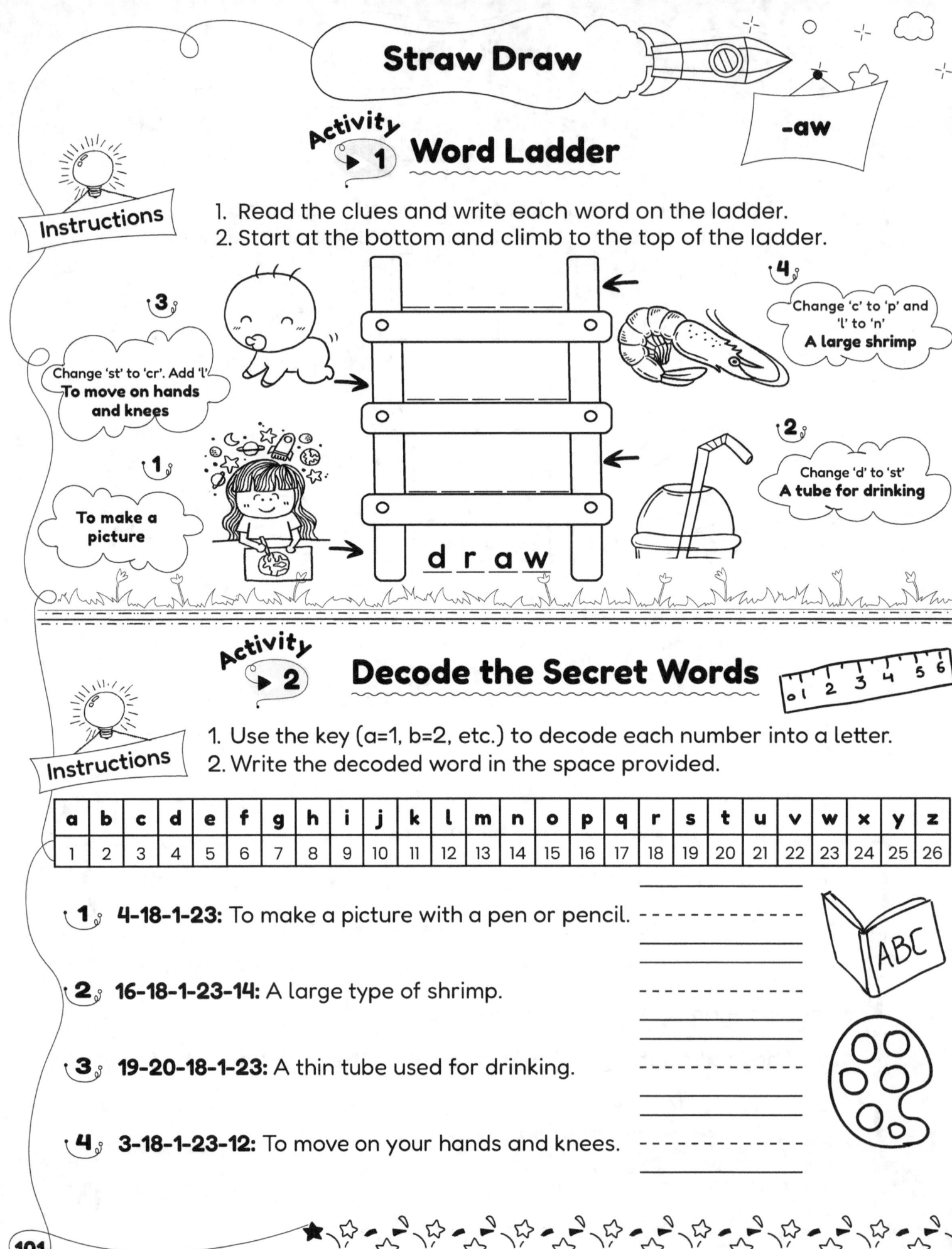

3 Change 'st' to 'cr'. Add 'l'
To move on hands and knees

4 Change 'c' to 'p' and 'l' to 'n'
A large shrimp

1 **To make a picture**

2 Change 'd' to 'st'
A tube for drinking

d r a w

Activity 2 — Decode the Secret Words

Instructions

1. Use the key (a=1, b=2, etc.) to decode each number into a letter.
2. Write the decoded word in the space provided.

a	b	c	d	e	f	g	h	i	j	k	l	m	n	o	p	q	r	s	t	u	v	w	x	y	z
1	2	3	4	5	6	7	8	9	10	11	12	13	14	15	16	17	18	19	20	21	22	23	24	25	26

1 **4-18-1-23:** To make a picture with a pen or pencil. - - - - - - - - - - - - -

2 **16-18-1-23-14:** A large type of shrimp. - - - - - - - - - - - - -

3 **19-20-18-1-23:** A thin tube used for drinking. - - - - - - - - - - - - -

4 **3-18-1-23-12:** To move on your hands and knees. - - - - - - - - - - - - -

-OW

Activity ▶1 Word Ladder

1. Read the clues and write each word on the ladder.
2. Start at the bottom and climb to the top of the ladder.

3 Change 'c' to 'b'
A color for tan

4 Change 'b' to 'f'
You're unhappy

1 **A funny person**

2 Change 'l' to 'r'
A headpiece

c l o w n

Activity ▶2 Alphabetical Order Exercises

1. Look at the list of words from the word ladder.
2. Write the words in alphabetical order in the spaces provided.

1 _ _ _ _ _ _ _ _ _ _ _ _

2 _ _ _ _ _ _ _ _ _ _ _ _

3 _ _ _ _ _ _ _ _ _ _ _ _

4 _ _ _ _ _ _ _ _ _ _ _ _

Word Bank
clown
frown
brown
crown

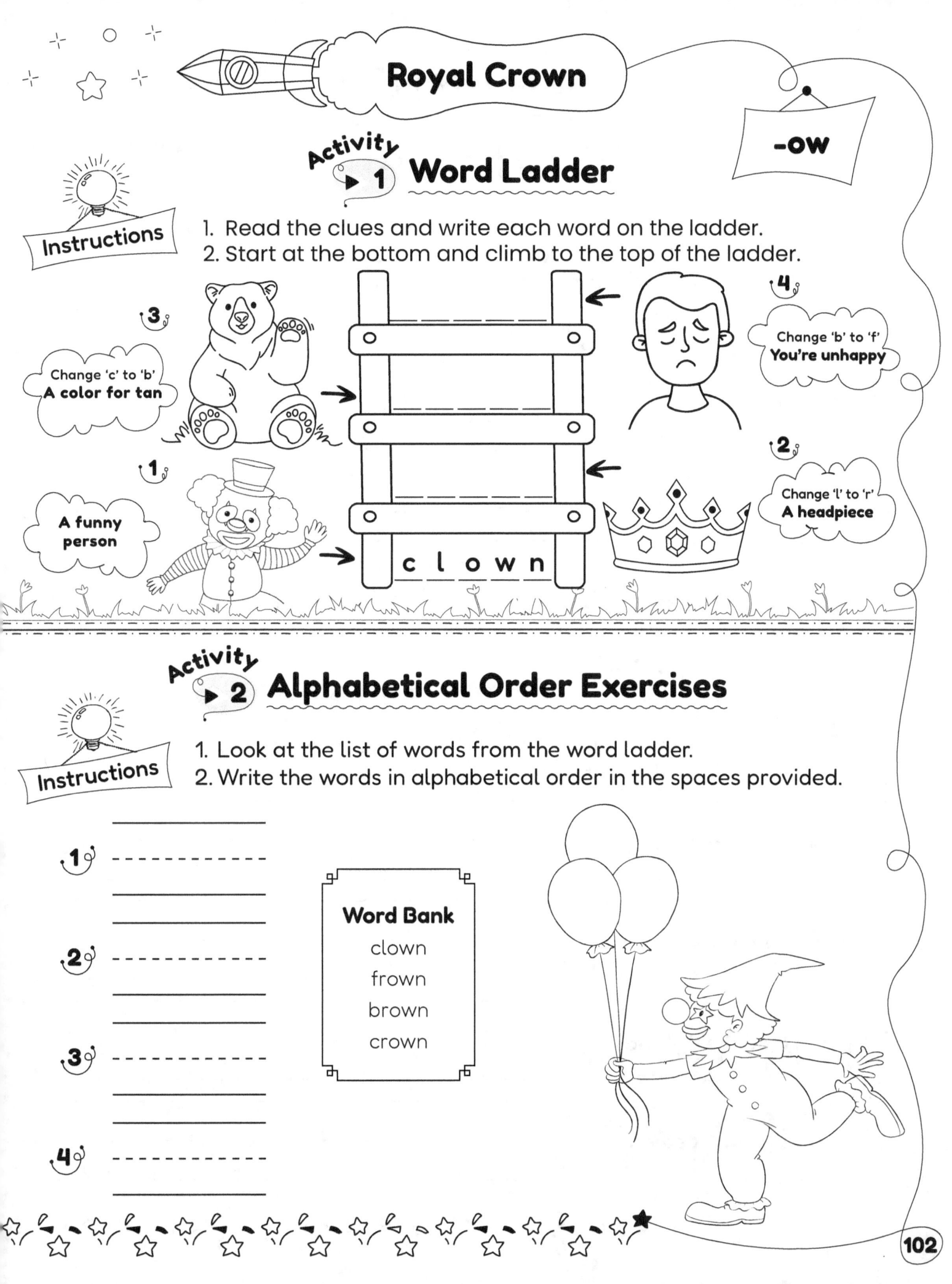

Bang and Hang Fun

Activity 1 — Word Ladder

-ang

Instructions

1. Read the clues and write each word on the ladder.
2. Start at the bottom and climb to the top of the ladder.

3 Change 'h' to 'f'
A long, sharp tooth

4 Change 'f' to 'g'
A group of people

1 A loud noise

2 Change 'b' to 'h'
To attach something from above

b a n g

Activity 2 — Sentence Scramble

Instructions

1. Unscramble the words to form correct sentences.
2. Write the sentences on the lines provided.

1 bang heard I a loud.

_____

2 hang clothes the to dry.

_____

3 sharp fang the tiger has.

_____

4 ate gang the together.

_____

Sing and Ring Tunes

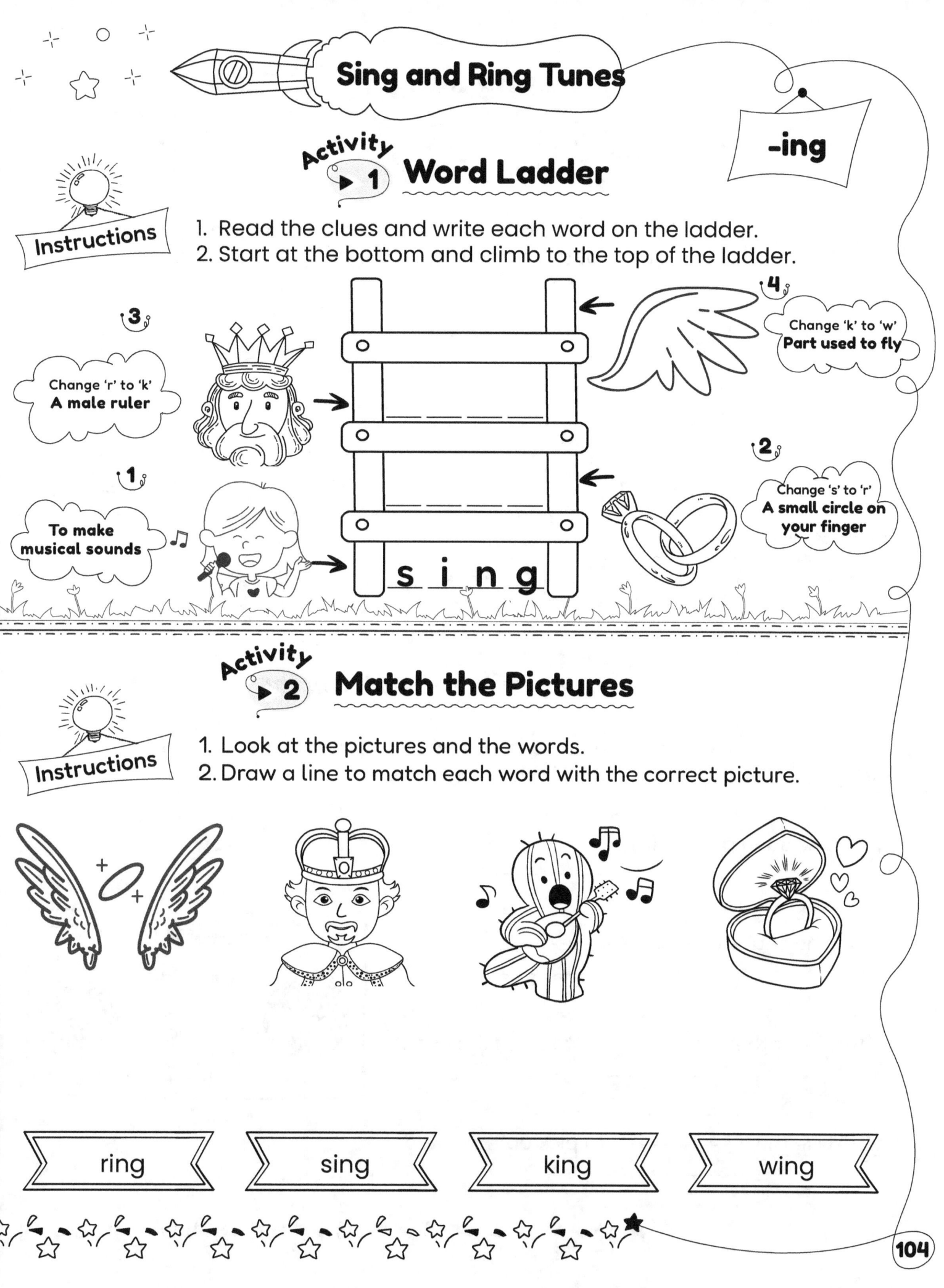

Activity ▶1 Word Ladder

-ing

Instructions
1. Read the clues and write each word on the ladder.
2. Start at the bottom and climb to the top of the ladder.

4 Change 'k' to 'w'
Part used to fly

3 Change 'r' to 'k'
A male ruler

2 Change 's' to 'r'
A small circle on your finger

1 To make musical sounds

s i n g

Activity ▶2 Match the Pictures

Instructions
1. Look at the pictures and the words.
2. Draw a line to match each word with the correct picture.

| ring | sing | king | wing |

Long Song

Activity 1 Word Ladder

Instructions
1. Read the clues and write each word on the ladder.
2. Start at the bottom and climb to the top of the ladder.

4 Change 'g' to 't' — A tool used to pick things up

3 Change 'l' to 'g' — A large metal disc

2 Change 's' to 'l' — Measuring a great distance

1 A piece of music with words

s o n g

Activity 2 Fill in the Blanks

Instructions
1. Complete each sentence with a word from the word bank.
2. Write the word in the blank space.

1 She sang a beautiful _____ .

2 The snake was very _____ .

3 He hit the _____ to start the event.

4 Use the _____ to pick up the salad.

Word Bank
tong
gong
song
long

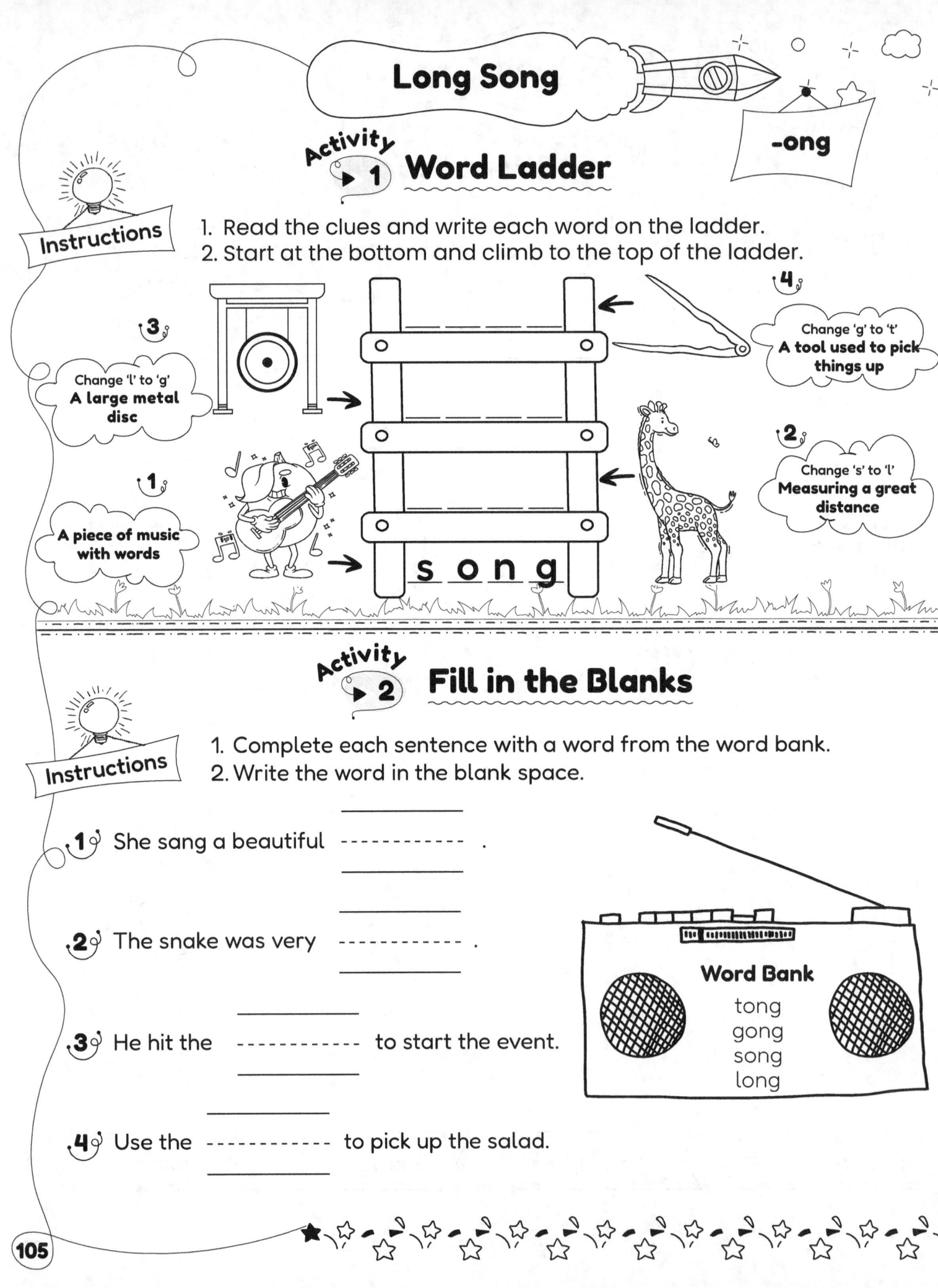

Stung in the Lung

Activity 1 Word Ladder

Instructions
1. Read the clues and write each word on the ladder.
2. Start at the bottom and climb to the top of the ladder.

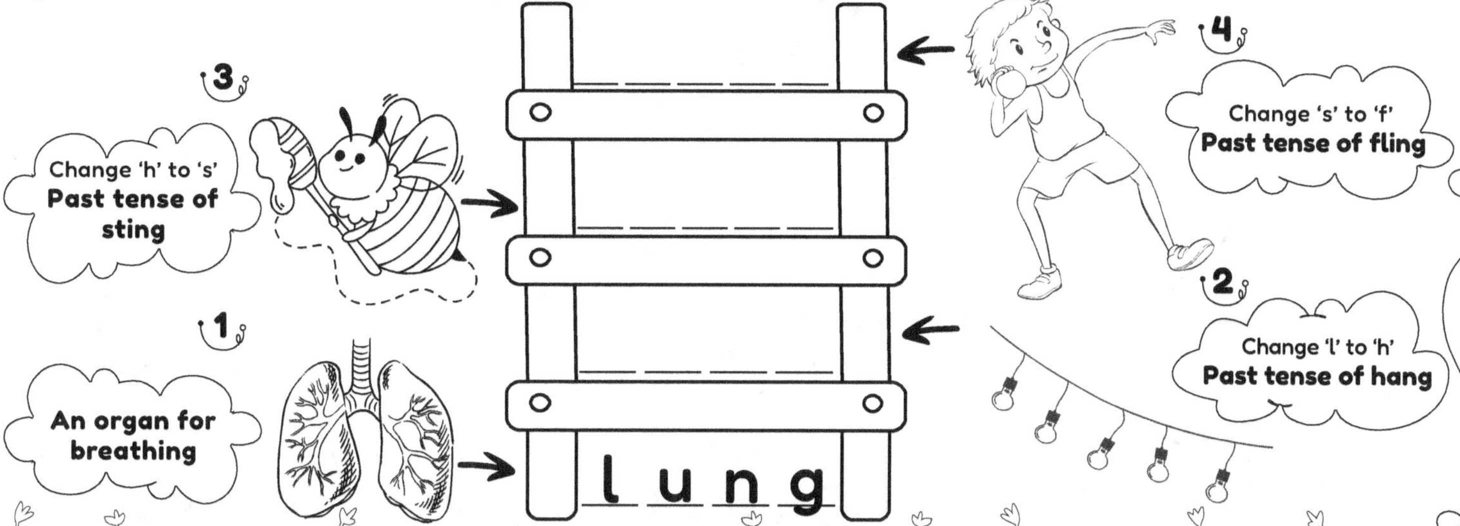

3
Change 'h' to 's'
Past tense of sting

4
Change 's' to 'f'
Past tense of fling

1
An organ for breathing

2
Change 'l' to 'h'
Past tense of hang

l u n g

Activity 2 Sort Words into Categories

Instructions
Write each word in the correct category.

-ung	Word Bank	-ing
	string	
	hung	
	lung	
	bring	
	stung	
	sling	
	flung	

Fun Printable Coloring Book!

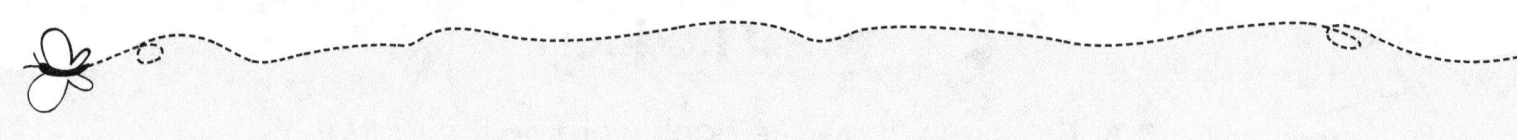

Could you spare just a minute?

Our biggest joy comes from helping little ones flourish and discover the world around them through learning.

That's why your thoughts matter so much to us!

Your honest thoughts about our book, even a quick sentence or two, would mean the world. We really mean it!

You'd be making a big difference for a small education brand like ours, run with love by a mother-daughter team.

Your reviews help us reach more curious minds across the globe, paving their way to success in their educational journey.

And hey, maybe we'll even sell a few more books in the process!

Every single review makes our hearts swell with gratitude.

Ready to make our day?

Scan the QR Code below to share your thoughts.

SCAN ME